NOTABLE WOMEN OF
MODERN CHINA

MARGARET E. BURTON

Author of "The Education of Women in China"

NOTABLE WOMEN OF MODERN CHINA

BIBLIOBAZAAR

NOTABLE WOMEN OF MODERN CHINA

Notable Women of Modern China

The author's earlier work on the general subject of Women's Education in China, indicates her ability to treat with peculiar interest and discernment the characters making up this volume of striking biographies. If these women are types to be followed by a great company of like aspirations the future of a nation is assured.

The Education of Women in China

"Thrilling is a strong word, but not too strong to be used in connection with *The Education of Women in China.* To many it will prove a revealing book and doubtless to all, even those well-informed upon the present condition of women. Miss Burton's book will interest all the reading public."—CHRISTIAN ADVOCATE.

Dr. Hü King Eng at the Time of Her Graduation
from the Medical College

TO MY FRIEND

GRACE COPPOCK

WHO TAUGHT ME TO KNOW AND
LOVE THE WOMEN OF CHINA

PREFACE

During a stay of some months in China in the year of 1909, I had an opportunity to see something of the educational work for women, and to meet several of the educated women of that interesting country. I was greatly impressed, both by the excellent work done by the students in the schools, and by the useful, efficient lives of those who had completed their course of study. When I returned to America, and spoke of some of the things which the educated women of China were doing, I found that many people were greatly surprised to learn that Chinese women were capable of such achievements. It occurred to me, therefore, that it might be worth while to put the stories of a few of these women into a form which would make them accessible to the public.

It will be noted that the majority of the women of whose work I have written received a part of their education in America. My reason for selecting these women is not because those whose training has been received wholly in China are not doing equally good work, but because it is difficult to gather definite information in regard to the women whose lives have been spent entirely in their native country. The fact that most of the biographies in this book are of women in professional life is due to the same cause. The great aim of the girls' schools in China is, rightly, to furnish such training as shall prepare their students to be worthy wives and mothers, and the large majority of those who attend the schools find their highest subsequent usefulness in the home. But in China, as in other countries, the life of the woman in the home remains, for the most part, unwritten.

I have therefore told the stories of the women concerning whose work I have been able to obtain definite information, believing that they fairly represent the educated women of China who, wherever their education has been received, and in whatever sphere it is being used, are ably and bravely playing an important part in the moulding of the great new China.

For much of the material for these sketches I am indebted to friends of the women of whom I have written. To all such my hearty thanks are due. For personal reminiscences, letters, and photographs, I am most grateful.

M. E. B.

CONTENTS

DR. HÜ KING ENG

MRS. AHOK

DR. IDA KAHN

DR. MARY STONE

ANNA STONE

ILLUSTRATIONS

DR. HÜ KING ENG

I

CHILDHOOD IN A CHRISTIAN HOME

Among the earliest converts to Christianity in South China was Hü Yong Mi, the son of a military mandarin of Foochow. He had been a very devout Buddhist, whose struggles after spiritual peace, and whose efforts to obtain it through fasting, sacrifice, earnest study, and the most scrupulous obedience to all the forms of Buddhist worship, remind one strongly of the experiences of Saul of Tarsus. Like Saul too, Hü Yong Mi was, before his conversion, a vigorous and sincere opponent of Christianity. When his older brother became a Christian, Hü Yong Mi felt that his casting away of idols and abolishing of ancestral worship were crimes of such magnitude that the entire family "ought all with one heart to beat the drum and drive him from the house." He tells of finding a copy of the Bible in his father's bookcase one day, and how, in sudden rage, he tore it to pieces and threw the fragments on the floor, and then, not satisfied with destroying the book, wished that he had some sharp implement with which to cut out "the hated name Ya-su, which stared from the mutilated pages."

But when, through the efforts of the very brother whom he had persecuted, he too came to recognize the truth of Christianity, he became as devoted and tireless a worker for his Lord as was Paul the apostle, preaching in season and out of season, first as a layman, afterwards as an ordained minister of the Methodist Church. His work often led him to isolated and difficult fields; he was "in journeyings often, in perils of rivers, in perils of robbers, in perils from his countrymen, in perils in the city, in perils in the wilderness." But, alike in toil and persecution, he remained steadfast.

He was made a presiding elder at the time of the organization of the Foochow Conference in 1877, and from that time until his death, in 1893, he was, in the words of one of the missionaries of that district, "a pillar of strength in the church in China, because of his piety and wisdom and his literary ability, having, withal, an eloquent tongue which in the ardour of pulpit oratory gave to his fine six-foot physique a princely bearing."

A striking testimony to the power and beauty of this Christian man's character is a picture, painted by a Chinese artist, an old man over eighty years of age. This man was not a Christian, but after hearing Mr. Hü's preaching, and watching his consecrated life, he embodied in a painting his conception of the power of the "Cross Doctrine" as he knew it through Hü Yong Mi. The picture, which is five feet long and nearly three wide, and is finely executed in water colours, was presented to Mr. Hü by the artist. At first glance its central figure seems to be a tree, under which is a man reading from a book. Lower down are some rocks. But looking again one sees that the tree is a cross, and that in the rocks are plain semblances of human faces, more or less perfect, all turned toward the cross. The thought which the artist wished to express was that the "Cross Doctrine," as preached and lived by such as Hü Yong Mi, would turn even rocks into human beings.

The wife of Hü Yong Mi was brought up in a home of wealth and rank in Foochow. Her aristocratic birth was manifested by the size of her tiny embroidered shoe, which measured exactly three inches. When Hü Yong Mi was asked by the missionaries to become a minister, he was somewhat dismayed to learn that in the Methodist Church the minister's family must frequently move from place to place. In his own words, "The Chinese greatly esteem the place of their birth; if a man goes abroad it is considered a matter of affliction; for a family to move is an almost unheard of calamity." He replied, however, that although he had not known of the existence of the custom, he was entirely willing, for Christ's sake, to undertake the work of a minister in spite of it. The missionaries then asked if his wife would be willing to go with him. He answered that he could not tell until he went home and asked her. But when he had talked the matter over with her, this dainty, high-class lady replied, "It matters not to what place; if you are willing to go, I will go with you."

Within a few weeks they left Foochow to work among their first parishioners, a people who might well have caused the hearts of the young pastor and his wife to fail, for Hü Yong Mi says of them: "In front of their houses I saw piles of refuse, and filthy ditches. Within, all was very dirty—pigs, cattle, fowls, sheep, all together in the one house. Not a chair was there to sit on. All went out to work in the fields. They had no leisure to comb hair or wash faces . . . None knew how to read the Chinese characters. Some held their books upside down; some mistook a whole column for one character." Mrs. Hü and the children were very ill with malarial fever while in this place, but in spite of all their hardships, a good work was done.

Mrs. Hü was as earnest a worker among the women as was her husband among the men, telling the good news to those who had never heard it, and strengthening her fellow-Christians. Many a programme of the Foochow Women's Conference bears the name of Mrs. Hü Yong Mi, for she could give addresses and read papers which were an inspiration to missionaries and Chinese alike. Her friend, Mrs. Sites, has written especially of her influence on the women whose lives she touched: "In the stations where the Methodist itinerancy sent Rev. Hü Yong Mi, this Christian household was something of a curiosity. The neighbouring women often called 'to see' in companies of three to twenty or more, and Mr. Hü expected his wife and children to preach the gospel to them just as faithfully as he did from the pulpit. There are many hundreds of Chinese women to whom this lovely Christian mother and little daughters gave the first knowledge of Christ and heaven." The same friend says of this wife and mother, "In privations oft, and in persecutions beyond the power of pen to narrate, she has become a model woman among her people."

In 1865, not long after a period of severe persecution, and while their hearts were saddened by the recent death of their little daughter, Hiong Kwang, another baby girl was born to Mr. and Mrs. Hü, and named Precious Peace, the Chinese for which is King Eng. Born of such parents, and growing up in such an environment, it is perhaps not surprising that unselfishness, steadfastness of purpose, and courage, both physical and moral, should be among the most prominent characteristics of Hü King Eng. One of the clearest memories of her childhood is of lying in bed night after night, listening to the murmur of her father's voice as he talked to someone who was interested in learning of the "Jesus way," and hearing the crash of stones and brickbats, the hurling of which through the doors and windows was too frequent an occurrence to interrupt these quiet talks.

Of course little King Eng's feet were bound, as were the feet of every other little girl of good family. But the binding process had scarcely begun when her father became convinced that this universal and ancient custom was a wrong one. He accordingly made the brave decision, unprecedented in that section of the country, that his daughters should have natural feet, and the bandages were taken off. This proceeding was viewed with great disapproval by his small daughter, for while it freed her from physical pain, her unbound feet were the source of constant comment and ridicule, far more galling to the sensitive child than the tight bandages had been. Now, an ardent advocate of natural feet, she often tells of her trials as a pioneer of the movement in Fuhkien province. "That I have the distinction of being the first girl who did not have her feet bound, is due to no effort of mine," she says, "for the neighbour women used to say, 'Rather a nice girl, but those feet!' 'Rather a bright girl, but those feet,' and 'Those feet,' 'Those feet' was all I heard, until I was ashamed to be seen."

Finally her mother, who did not wholly share her husband's view of the matter, took advantage of his absence from home, and replaced the bandages. When she would ask, "Can you stand them a little tighter?" the little devotee to the stern mandates of fashion and custom invariably replied, "Yes, mother, a little tighter"; for was she not going to be a lady and not hear "those feet," "those feet" any more! But when her father came home he had a long and serious talk with his wife about foot-binding, and off came the bandages again. Later the little girl went on a visit to a relative, who was greatly horrified at her large feet, and took it upon herself to bind them again, to the child's great delight. It was with an immense sense of her importance that she came hobbling home, supported on each side. Her mother was ill in bed at the time, but greatly to King Eng's disappointment, instead of being pleased, she bade her take the bandages off and burn them, and never replace them. To the child's plea that people were all saying "those feet," "those feet," until she was ashamed to meet any one, Mrs. Hü replied,

"Tell them bound-footed girls never enter the emperor's palace."
"And that," says Dr. Hü, "put a quietus on 'those feet,' and when I learned that all the world did not have bound feet I became more reconciled."

II

EDUCATION IN CHINA AND AMERICA

When she was old enough, King Eng became a pupil in the Foochow Boarding School for Girls, where she did good work as a student. No musical teaching was given in the school at that time, but King Eng was so eager to learn to play that the wife of one of the missionaries gave her lessons on her own organ. Her ability to play may have been one of the causes which led to the framing of a remarkable and eloquent appeal for the higher education of the Chinese girls, which should include music and English, sent in 1883 by the native pastors of Foochow and vicinity to the General Executive Committee of the Woman's Foreign Missionary Society of the Methodist Episcopal Church, under whose auspices this school was carried on.

To the same committee there came at the same time another remarkable request, this one from Dr. Trask, then in charge of the Foochow Woman's Hospital. After leaving boarding school King Eng had been a student in the hospital, and Dr. Trask had become so much impressed with her adaptability to medical work, and her sympathetic spirit toward the suffering, that she longed to have her receive the advantages of a more thorough education than could be given her in Foochow. She accordingly wrote to the Executive Committee of the Woman's Foreign Missionary Society, speaking in the highest terms of Hü King Eng's ability and character, and urging that arrangements be made to bring her to America, to remain ten years if necessary, "that she might go back qualified to lift the womanhood of China to a higher plane, and able to superintend the medical work." She assured the committee that they would find that the results would justify them in doing this, and that none knew King Eng but to love her. Arrangements were soon made, largely through Mrs. Keen, secretary of the Philadelphia branch of the Woman's Foreign Missionary Society, and word was sent to Foochow that Dr. Trask's request had been approved.

This word found Hü King Eng ready to accept the opportunity which it offered her. It had not been easy for this young girl, only eighteen years old, to decide to leave her home and her country and take the long journey to a foreign land, whose language she could not speak, and whose customs were utterly strange to her, to remain there long enough to receive the college and medical education which would enable her to do the work planned for her on her return to China. So far as she knew she was the only Chinese young woman who had ever left China to seek an education in another country; and indeed she was the second, the only one who had preceded her being Dr. You Mé King, the adopted daughter of Dr. and Mrs. McCartee, of Ningpo, who had gone to America with them a few years before. King Eng's parents did not oppose her going, but neither did they encourage it. They told her fully of the loneliness she would experience in a foreign country; the dangers and unpleasantness of the long ocean voyage she would have to take; and the unparalleled situation in which she would find herself on her return ten years later, unmarried at twenty-eight. But with a quiet faith and purpose, and a courage nothing short of heroic, King Eng answered, "If the Lord opens the way and the cablegram says 'Come,' I shall surely go; but if otherwise I shall do as best I can and labour at home."

Years afterward, when two other girls from the Foochow Boarding School were leaving China for a period of study in America, a farewell meeting was held for them in the school, at which Dr. Hü told how she had reached her decision to go. She said: "I was the first Fuhkien province girl to go to America ... My father told me, 'I cannot decide for you; you must pray to God. If you are to go, God will show you.' Then I felt God's word come to me, 'Fear not, for I will go with you wherever you go.' At that time the school girls were seldom with the missionary ladies and I could not speak any English, therefore I did not know any American politeness; and all my clothes and other daily-need-things were not proper to use in the western country. Although everything could not be according to my will, I trusted God with all my life, so nothing could change my heart."

In the spring of 1884, in charge of some missionaries going home on furlough, Hü King Eng left China for America. The journey was a long and rough one, and a steamer near theirs was wrecked. One of the missionaries, wondering how her faith was standing the test of these new and terrifying experiences, asked if she wanted to go back home. But she answered, "No, I do not think of going home at all." She felt that it was right for her to go to America, and although when she met her friends at the journey's end she confessed that sea-sickness and home-sickness had brought the tears many a night, she never faltered in her decision.

Upon landing in New York she went at once to Mrs. Keen in Philadelphia, and there met Dr. and Mrs. Sites, of Foochow, whom she had known from childhood, and who were then in Philadelphia attending the General Conference of the Methodist Church. She spent the summer with them, learning to read, write, and speak English, and in the autumn went with them to Delaware, Ohio, and entered Ohio Wesleyan University. Miss Martin, who was then preceptress of Monnett Hall, recalls King Eng's efforts to master English. "She was an apt pupil," she says, "yet she had many struggles with the language." A friend in Cleveland, with whom she spent a few weeks during her vacation, promised her that some day they would go around the square to see the reservoir. King Eng seemed much interested in this proposition and several times asked when they were to go. When they finally went, her friend was somewhat surprised to see that King Eng manifested very little interest in the reservoir; but when they reached home again it was evident that she had been interested, not in the reservoir, but in the proposed method of reaching it. "How can you go 'round' a 'square'?" she asked.

When she entered college she set herself the task of learning ten new words a day; but Miss Martin says that she sometimes had to unlearn several of them, owing to the fondness of her fellow students for slang. However, she was persevering, and in time learned to use the language easily. One of the teachers, who had returned a plate to her with an orange on it, still treasures a half sheet of paper which appeared on a returned plate of hers, on which King Eng had written:

"You taught me a lesson not long ago,
Which I have learned, as I'll try to show.
When you would return a plate to its owner,
Of something upon it you must be the donor.
One orange you put on that plate of mine,
Two oranges find on this plate of thine."

She was a great favourite with both faculty and students. One of her fellow students shall tell of the impression she made: "Those who were at Monnett Hall at any time from 1884 to 1887 will remember a dainty little foreign lady, a sort of exotic blossom, whose silk-embroidered costumes, constructed in Chinese fashion, made her an object of interest to every girl in college. This was Dr. Hü King Eng, who came to prepare for her life work. Gentle, modest, winning, her heart fixed on a goal far ahead, she was an example to the earnest Christian girl and a rebuke to any who had self-seeking aims."

Another, looking back to her college days, and to the college life of Hü King Eng, "or, as she was familiarly and lovingly called, King Eng," writes, "She was so sweet and gracious, so simple in her faith and life, so charitable, that you felt it everywhere. I shall never forget standing in the hall one day with her and another girl, when a young man delivered some books. I asked his name. The young lady gave it, a well known name, and added that he had very little principle, or character. King Eng spoke up at once, and calling the other girl by name said, 'Yes, but his parents are fine people.'"

The King's Daughters' Society was organized during King Eng's stay at Ohio Wesleyan, and ten groups, of ten girls each, were formed among the students of Monnett Hall. King Eng, who was the leader of one of these groups, proposed that each girl in it should earn enough money to buy one of the King's Daughters' badges, and that they should be sent to some of the girls in the Foochow school, that they too might organize a society. She was eager that the girls should not only give the badges, but should earn them by their own efforts, that they might thus show the Chinese girls that American students did not consider any kind of work beneath them, but counted it an honour to serve their Master in any way possible.

During the April of King Eng's first year at Ohio Wesleyan University, special meetings were held in connection with the Day of Prayer for Colleges, one of them a large chapel service at which the president of the college and the preceptress spoke. The report of this meeting shows that King Eng did not wait until her return to China to begin active efforts to win others to the Christian life. "At the close of an address by Miss Martin, the preceptress, there stepped forward upon the rostrum our little Chinese student, Miss Hü King Eng, who, dressed in her full native costume, stood gracefully before these six hundred young men and women while she witnessed to the saving power of Christ . . . The following evening, at our earnest revival service in the chapel of the ladies' boarding hall, there knelt the Chinese girl at the side of her American sister, helping her to find the Saviour; and the smile of gladness on her countenance at the closing of the meeting told the joy in her heart because her friend was converted. The faith of many has been made stronger by hearing the testimony of Miss Hü."

The statement of one of her fellow students is impressive: "She had a great influence over the girls, and during our revival seasons she usually led more to Christ than any other girl in the school. One mother, when she came to visit the school after such a meeting during which her own daughter had been converted, exclaimed, 'Little did I think when I was giving money for the work in China, that a Chinese girl would come to this country and be the means of leading my daughter to Christ.'"

Miss Martin tells of one student who had long resisted all appeals, but who would listen to King Eng when she would not hear any one else; and who was finally led by her to such a complete consecration that she afterward gave her life to missionary service in Japan.

During her vacation periods King Eng often addressed missionary meetings with marked success, winning such testimonies as these: "We are thanking God for that grand missionary meeting. It would have done your heart good to have heard the references to it in our Wednesday night prayer meeting," or, "One gentleman said to me, 'That was the best missionary meeting we ever had in Third Avenue.'" It was probably while doing such work as this that she had the experiences which led her to realize so keenly the blessing of the unbound feet which had caused her so many tribulations as a child, for she says that when she was running for trains in America she always remembered "Those feet," "Those feet," and was glad that she had them.

In the summer of 1886 she attended a meeting of the International Missionary Union, and there met Mrs. Baldwin, who had known her as a child in Foochow. Mrs. Baldwin wrote of the impression she made at this time: "Our dear little Chinese girl, Hü King Eng, won all hearts, as usual, by her sweet, gentle, trustful Christian character. To us who have known her from her infancy up, the meeting was of peculiar pleasure; and as she grasped my hand and in low, earnest, glad tones exclaimed in our Foochow dialect, 'Teacheress, all the same as seeing my own house people,' I could heartily respond, 'All the same.'"

At the same time she was making rapid progress in her studies. At the annual meeting of the Woman's Foreign Missionary Society in 1886, "the marvellous progress of Hü King Eng was reported . . . and tears of gladness filled many eyes as her implicit faith, her sturdy industry, and her untiring devotion were described."

She completed her course in Ohio Wesleyan University in four years, and in the autumn of 1888 entered the Woman's Medical College of Philadelphia, doing the regular class work, and making her home with her friend Mrs. Keen. After two years of work there, she was very ill with a fever for many weeks. When her strength began to come back, it was decided that she should stop studying for a time and go to China for the following year, as she was very eager to visit her home, especially as her father was ill. Her lifelong friend, Miss Ruth Sites, was also returning to Foochow at that time. So after securing a passport for Hü King Eng, in order that she might be able to return to America, the two girls made the trip together, spending Christmas in Yokohama, and enjoying a short visit to Tokio. The steamer stopped for a day at Kobe, and there Miss Hü had the pleasure of visiting Dr. You Mé King, then practising medicine under the Southern Methodist Mission. Dr. You was the only Chinese woman who had ever left China for study up to the time of her own going. They had a day at Nagasaki also, where several college mates from Ohio Wesleyan were working; and two days were spent in Shanghai, during which Miss Hü visited Dr. Reifsnyder's splendid hospital. The trip from Shanghai to Foochow was the last part of the long journey, and they were soon in the quiet waters of the Min River. Miss Sites, writing back to America, said that she could never forget King Eng's look as she exclaimed, "The last wave is past. Now we are almost home." A brother and a brother-in-law came several miles down the river in a launch to meet her, and sedan chairs were waiting at the landing to take her to her home, where her parents were eagerly awaiting her. A reception of welcome was given for her and Miss Sites a few days later, which was for her father and mother one of the proudest occasions of their lives.

Some of the missionaries had wondered whether so many years of residence in America would not have changed King Eng, and whether some of the luxuries she had enjoyed there might not have become a necessity to her. With this in mind many little comforts unusual in a Chinese home had been put into her room. "But," one of them writes, "this was needless." King Eng was unchanged and all the attention she had received in America had left her unspoiled. This was doubtless largely due to the purity of her purpose in going. In bidding good-bye, a few years later, to some girls who were going to America for the first time, she said: "Some people do not want girls to go to America to study because they think when the girls are educated they will be proud. I think really we have nothing to be proud of. We Chinese girls have such a good opportunity to go to another country to study, not because God loves us better than any other persons, but because He loves *all* our people in China. Therefore He sends us to learn all the good things first, so that we may help our people. The more favour we receive the more debt we owe the Chinese women and girls. So wherever we go we must think how to benefit our people, and not do as we please, and then how can we be proud?"

The only cloud in this happy home-coming, after eight years of absence, was the illness of her father, who was suffering from consumption. But even this cloud was lightened by the help and cheer which King Eng was enabled to bring to him. Miss Sites wrote: "It is an unspeakable comfort to him to have King Eng with him, while she, with skill and wisdom learned in Philadelphia, attends to all his wants as no other Chinese could." Soon after King Eng's return her father was prostrated with a severe attack of grippe, which in his already weakened state, made his condition almost hopeless. Even the missionary doctor who attended him had no expectation that he would recover. "But," reads a letter from Mrs. Sites, "through the knowledge King Eng had acquired of caring for the sick, and her devotion to her father, with work unfaltering, and prayer unceasing, he was brought back to us."

For many years Rev. Hü Yong Mi had been planning to build a house, wherein he and his family might live after he was too feeble to preach, and which his family might have if he should be taken from them. At this time he had laid by enough money to carry out his plan, but his weakness was such that he could have done little, had it not been for the energy and vigour of his wide-awake daughter. She helped make the plans for the house, and afterward urged forward the building, so that a few months after her return the family moved out of the parsonage into a comfortable little home, built in Chinese style, but with glass windows and board floors.

In addition to the care of her father and the superintendence of the building of the new house, King Eng was kept very busy in the hospital, interpreting for the physicians in the daily clinics, and working among the in-patients. This experience was invaluable to her at this time in giving her a clearer knowledge of the especial preparation needed in her future work. She saw and learned much of the prevalent diseases among the women for whom she was preparing herself to work. She also taught a class of young women medical students, which gave her valuable experience in that line of work.

One of the missionaries has written of the impression she made during this stay in Foochow: "She was kept very busy in the hospital and her home, but she was always cheerful and helpful. Her Christian love and natural kindness drew to her the hearts of hundreds of suffering native women, who felt that there was sympathy for them in her every look and touch. Moreover, the affectionate regard in which she had been held by her missionary associates in Foochow has been vastly increased by her unassuming manner, and the meek and quiet spirit in which she mingled with us in work and prayer through the months."

The new home was beautifully situated, overlooking the river and receiving constant south breezes, which made it cool and comfortable in summer. It was hoped that in its quiet Mr. Hü might live for a number of years, and it was therefore decided that King

Eng should return to America, to re-enter the Woman's Medical College of Philadelphia in the fall of 1892. On the return trip she said to Mrs. Sites, who was with her, "I have learned to trust God fully, else how could I be going away from my sick father whose every move and cough I had learned to hear so quickly through all the hours of the night, and still my heart be at rest?" Mrs. Sites adds, "Personally, her companionship on the voyage was a continual joy to me, notwithstanding my alarming and wearisome struggle while in Montreal to get permission for her to re-enter this alarmingly exclusive country."

Hü King Eng re-entered the Medical College in the autumn of 1892, graduating with honour the eighth of May, 1894. She spent the following year in hospital work, being fortunate enough to be chosen as surgeon's assistant in the Philadelphia Polyclinic, which gave her the privilege of attending all the clinics and lectures there.

III

BEGINNING MEDICAL WORK IN CHINA

In 1895 Dr. Hü returned to Foochow. She at once began work in the Foochow Hospital for women and children, being associated with Dr. Lyon, who wrote at the end of the year's work: "Dr. Hü, by her faithfulness and skill, has built up the dispensary until the number of the patients treated far exceeds that of last year. She has also been a great inspiration to our students, not only as teacher, but in right living and in Christian principles." The following year Dr. Lyon returned to America on her furlough, leaving the young physician in entire charge of the hospital work, a responsibility which she discharged so effectively that at the close of the year her co-labourers enthusiastically declared: "Sending Hü King Eng to America for a medical education was providing for one of the greatest blessings that ever came to Foochow. Skilled in her profession, kind and patient, Christlike in spirit, one of their very own, her influence cannot be measured."

At about this time Dr. Hü was honoured by being appointed by His Excellency, Li Hung Chang, as one of the two delegates from China to the Women's Congress held in London in 1898. But she was very seriously ill with pneumonia that year, and for weeks it was feared that she could not recover. A letter from Mrs. Lacy, then living in Foochow, reads: "Dr. Hü King Eng has been lying at the gates of death for nearly three weeks. Dr. Lyon said she was beyond all human aid. Most earnest and constant prayers by the native Christians have been offered in her behalf. We are glad to report a decided improvement in her condition although she is by no means out of danger yet. Dr. Hü is a very valuable worker, not only a most successful physician, but a very superior instructor in medicine, and is very greatly beloved by both natives and foreigners, and it does not seem as if she could be spared. We can but believe that God is going to honour the faith of His children and raise her up to do yet greater service for Him."

Gradually health and strength came back, and the next year it was reported that Dr. Hü had sufficiently recovered her health to teach one class in the Girls' Boarding School. A trip to the home of a married sister in Amoy, which gave her a sea voyage, and change of air and scene, completed her recovery and in 1899 she was strong enough to take charge of the Woolston Memorial Hospital.

Dr. Hü's Medical Students

The Foochow Hospital for women and children is situated on Nan Tai Island, three miles from the walled city of Foochow. The physicians had long felt the need of a similar work within the city walls, and a few years before Dr. Hü's return from America, work had been undertaken in the city. A small building was erected, in which forty in-patients could be accommodated. This little building was named the Woolston Memorial Hospital, and nurses from the Island hospital took turns in working in it, under the supervision of one of the physicians. But until Dr. Hü took charge of the work, in 1899, there had been no resident physician.

Some years later, in telling of her appointment to this work, Dr. Hü said: "It is very different from what I had heard of the city people being proud and hard to manage. I am glad God created Lot. If he did not help any one else he surely helped me. At the time I said nothing and went, simply because I did not want to be like Lot. No one knows how I shrank when I was asked to work in the city; for when I thought of the place, the pitiful picture of the Island hospital students would come most conspicuously before me. I can see them even now, wiping away the tears just as hard as they could when their turn came to go into the city; while the other students were like 'laughing Buddhas,' for their turn in the city hospital had expired. I am glad I can speak for myself to-day that in my five years' experience I have never had to shed a tear because the people were obstinate."

Nevertheless the first few months were not altogether easy ones. Dr. Hü herself tells the story of the beginnings of the work: "When I first took up my work in the city here, during the first few months what did I meet? People came and said that they wanted a foreign doctor. When our Bible woman told them that I had just returned from a foreign country, and that I knew foreign medicine, what was the immediate reply which I heard? 'No, I don't want a Chinese student, but I want a foreign doctor.' It made my Bible woman indignant, but by this time I usually stepped out and told them just where to go to find the foreign doctors. It surprised my hospital people that instead of feeling hurt I would do what I did."

It was only a few months, however, before the city people discovered that this "Chinese student" was a most valuable member of the community. By summer the work of the little hospital was so prosperous that Dr. Hü decided to keep the dispensary open for three mornings a week, even after the intense heat had necessitated the closing of the hospital proper. Some of the patients signified their approval of this decision by renting rooms in the neighbourhood, in order to be able to attend the dispensary on the open days.

During this first year of work in the Woolston Hospital Dr. Hü had two medical students in training, who also assisted her in the hospital work, one of them her younger sister, Hü Seuk Eng. She speaks warmly of their work among the patients, and of the patients' appreciation of what was done for them. "Very frequently," she wrote at the close of the year, "I hear the patients say, 'Truly my own parents, brothers, and sisters could never be so good, so patient, and do so carefully for us; especially when we are so filthy and foul in these sore places. Yes, this religion must be better than ours.'"

Thus, although the work was begun in fear and trembling, and the young physician had some obstacles to overcome, she treated 2,620 patients during the first year, and was able to report a most encouraging outlook at its close.

IV

THE BELOVED PHYSICIAN

As Dr. Hü's work grew it fell into four main divisions; the dispensary work, the work among the hospital patients, visits to the homes of those too ill to come to her, and the superintendence of the training of medical students. The city hospital has been crowded almost from the very outset. The situation was somewhat relieved in 1904, by the building of a house for Dr. Hü on Black Rock Hill. This enabled her to move out of the hospital and thus enlarged the space available for patients; but the additional space was soon filled and the building was as crowded as before. Dr. Hü is utilizing the building to the best possible advantage. One of her fellow missionaries writes that every department is as well arranged as in any hospital she has ever seen; every nook and corner is clean and tidy, students are happy, helpful, and studious, and patients are cared for both physically and spiritually.

The hospital records hold many a story of those who found both physical and spiritual healing during their stay there. One day a woman over fifty, whose husband and son had died while she was very young, came to the hospital for treatment. When she was only twenty-two, crushed by her grief, and feeling, as she said, that there was no more pleasure in this world for her, she made a solemn vow before the idols that she would be a vegetarian for the rest of her life, hoping in this way to obtain reward in the next life. At the time she came to the hospital she had kept this vow sacredly for nearly thirty years, being so scrupulous in her observance of it that she even used her own cooking utensils in the hospital, lest some particle of animal matter should have adhered to the others and thus contaminate her food. She was so unostentatious about it, however, that Dr. Hü did not know she was a vegetarian until she prescribed milk for her.

While in the hospital this woman was greatly surprised to hear, in morning prayers every day, that which she could but admit was better than her old belief. Day by day she compared the Christian teaching with her old religion, until finally one morning, after she had been in the hospital about a week, she went to Dr. Hü after the service, and said: "Doctor, your religion is better than mine. I want to be a Christian, but very unfortunately I have made a solemn vow to idols, and now, if I should change my faith, these idols would punish me, my children, and children's children." The doctor assured her that she need not be afraid, since the idols to which she had made her vow were only wood and stone, powerless to harm her. She went off comforted, and a few hours later she created tremendous excitement through the hospital by preparing and eating the first meal of meat she had had for almost thirty years. Some of the patients were much frightened, for the vegetarian vow is considered a most sacred one which, when broken, can never be made again, and they feared that some dire calamity would overtake her. Nothing worse occurred, however, than an attack of indigestion, the natural consequence of too free indulgence in the flesh pots after so many years of abstinence; and the dauntless old lady announced her intention of enjoying many a similar meal in the days to come.

Her home was at some distance, and after she left the hospital nothing more was seen of her until three years later, when she appeared one day, bringing with her several patients for treatment. She had gained so much flesh, and looked so well, that she had to tell the doctor who she was. She said that after she went home, and her vegetarian friends saw the dishes of meat on her table and realized that she had broken her sacred vow, they were indignant and alarmed, and would have nothing to do with her. But within the previous year some of them had gradually begun to come to see her again. "I felt badly for their ignorance," she said, "but, oh, I was very glad to have the opportunity to tell them of what you had told me when I was converted."

At one time a former patient of the doctor's, who belonged to a prominent family in the city, brought an old man of seventy-one for treatment. The rule of the hospital is that only women and children shall be received as in-patients, so the doctor directed him to go to Dr. Kinnear's hospital. But the old man looked greatly disappointed and begged pitifully: "I am a poor old man and my limb is very painful; *I-seng* (doctor), do help me and have mercy upon me. Do not look upon me as a man, but a child." The doctor's tender heart finally prevailed and she made an exception of him. When the old man was cured he came back to the hospital regularly, every day, for the morning service. After listening attentively for a few weeks, he said to the doctor, "*I-seng*, I truly know this is a good religion and is just what I want, and I have decided to bow down to this very God."

His health did not improve as rapidly as the doctor thought it should; and upon making careful inquiries she learned that it was because the small amount of money which it was possible for him to earn, was not sufficient to provide him with the nourishing food he needed. She at once gave him some money, telling him to buy the sort of food which would build-up his strength, and not to tell any one that he had been given this help. But this was altogether too much to ask of the grateful old man, and "he went out and began to publish it." The family who had sent him to the doctor were much touched by this fresh evidence of her kindness, and thereafter they sent their son with the old man to the morning services each day, saying: "The Christian doctor is so good and kind. She has not only treated this poor man free of charge but has helped him with money. Surely this religion must be good."

Often patients come from far away villages to enter the hospital. One young girl from a town many miles up the Min River, who became a happy, eager Christian in the hospital, went home with the hope of coming back to study in the Girls' Boarding School the next year. She was very eager to tell the people of her village, in the meantime, of the glad truths she had learned. "I will be the only Christian in the village," she said. "How I wish Dr. Hü and Lau Sing-sang Moing (the Bible woman) would come and tell my people about the new religion. I will tell them all I know, but I don't know very much." One case is related of an old woman with double cataracts, whose son brought her on a wheelbarrow a distance of several hundred miles to consult Dr. Hü. The doctor performed a successful operation, restoring the woman's sight, and thereby earning the title of "The Miracle Lady."

A large work is done every year in the dispensary, where Dr. Hü receives patients each morning. This work has grown from 1,837 cases the first year to 24,091 in 1910, and has made literally thousands of friends for the doctor and her work. When she planned to erect the little building in which she lives on Black Rock Hill many people told her that they were sure the priests, especially those of the Black Rock Hill temple, would strongly object to the erection of a mission building on that site, which was considered a particularly sacred one. But Dr. Hü felt no anxiety in regard to that, for the priests had been coming to the dispensary for treatment for some months previous to the time of beginning the building. "Some have come from Singapore monastery," she wrote, "others from Kushan, still others from those in our own city. Thank God that their illnesses were quickly healed."

She tells of one of the Singapore priests who was so grateful to be well again that he came to the hospital one morning, dressed as for some festival occasion, and bringing with him two boxes of cakes and two Chinese scrolls, the Chinese characters of which he had himself written. These he presented to Dr. Hü with his lowest bow, saying, "If I had not come to you and taken your medicine I would have been dead, or at least I would not be able to go back to Singapore." Many priests even came to the morning services and listened attentively to what was said there.

A somewhat incidental but very useful work carried on largely in the dispensary, by the Bible women, is a crusade against foot-binding. Dr. Hü's useful life, and the important part her strong, natural feet play in it, is a most effective object-lesson; and the annual reports usually record a goodly number of those who have unbound their feet during the year.

The most difficult part of the work is that of visiting the sick in their homes, both because of the great distances that have to be covered, and because in many cases the doctor is not called except as a last resort. One of Dr. Hü's reports reads: "I am very sorry that we do not yet have foreign vehicles, railroads, or street cars. It takes much time to go from one place to another. Fortunately my Chinese people live near together, with their relatives, so when I am invited to go to see one case I often have to prescribe for sixteen or twenty cases before my return." Often when the doctor answers a call she finds that the patient has been ill for a long time, while the relatives have been seeking to obtain help from the Chinese doctor or from idols. She herself shall tell the story of an experience of this kind:

> "Last week I was called to see a woman very ill with cholera. Her people had had all known doctors, both in and out of the city, and had consulted with and begged many idols to heal her, but the woman had grown worse and worse, until, when she was apparently hopeless, having been unconscious for two days, one of the doctors suggested to try me. I went at once, and found the room crowded with friends and relatives. They could not tell me fast enough what a good and filial woman she was, but that the idols had said certain spirits wanted her, and no amount of offerings could buy her back again. I told them that the woman was *very* ill, and that I feared it was too late for my medicine to help her. Many voices replied, 'We know, we know, and if she dies we will not blame you.' With a prayer, and three doses of medicine left for the woman to take, we left them."

> "That afternoon her husband came to report that she was better. I went to see her and to my great surprise she *was* better. While there a famous idol arrived to drive out the evil spirit. I said, 'Do you want me, or do you want the idols? We cannot work together.' They insisted that I continue to prepare my medicine and said that the idol could wait. He did wait twenty minutes, and I have been told since that no one ever dared to ask an idol to wait before. Before leaving they promised me that the idol should not go near, or do anything outrageous to the woman. This is now the tenth day and the woman seems to have quite recovered."

> "The woman's husband came yesterday and told me that not only he, but many friends and relatives, were convinced that the idols were false; for one idol would give one cause for the illness of his wife, and another idol would give another cause; while once they did not give the medicine sent by an idol and he (the medium) said later, 'The medicine has done her good.' The husband said, 'We see plainly that my wife was saved by your God, by you, and your medicine.'"

While Dr. Hü has done a great deal of work for the poor, her practice is by no means limited to that class, for she is often called to the homes of the official and wealthy classes. One grateful husband, whose wife and baby Dr. Hü had saved, told her that he would not only give money towards her new hospital himself, but would also help her to obtain subscriptions from his friends. "Chinese doctors have learned to use clinical thermometers," he observed, "but the Chinese medicine does not seem to fit the foreign thermometer, for the patients do not seem to get well as with the foreign medicine."

The first student to receive a diploma from the Woolston Memorial Hospital was Dr. Hü's sister, Hü Seuk Eng, who graduated in April, 1902. The graduation exercises, held in the Sing Bo Ting Ancestral Hall, which was willingly loaned for the occasion, created a keen interest, and numbers of the city people gathered to witness proceedings so unusual. Many of them said, "This is the first time a Christian service was ever held in a temple." But what was even more wonderful to them was the revelation of the possibilities of Chinese young womanhood which they received. Dr. Hü wrote that after the exercises an official who lived near by announced: "I will buy a girl seven or eight years old and I will have a tutor for her. Then I will send her to the Girls' Boarding School to study, and then she may go to Dr. Hü to study medicine. Then she will go to Sing Bo Ting Ancestral Temple, too, to receive her diploma. Besides, we will all be Christians." Others were heard to exclaim, "Who knew girls could do so much good to the world—more than our boys!"

When the exercises were over, greatly to Seuk Eng's surprise, her sedan chair was escorted all the way back to the hospital, to the accompaniment of the popping of hundreds of fire-crackers, set off in her honour. A Chinese feast was prepared for the guests in the hospital, after which another unexpected explosion of congratulatory fire-crackers took place. Thus ended in true Chinese fashion, amid noise and smoke, the first graduation exercises of the Woolston Memorial Hospital.

They were by no means the last, however, for this department of work has been steadily carried on ever since Dr. Hü took charge of the hospital. In 1904 she reported: "Our little medical school is getting on nicely. The success of the school is mostly due to our good teacher and the students themselves, who have a great desire to learn. They have had written examinations this year; the highest general average was 98 and the lowest 85. Can any one dare to think, 'What is the use to teach these Chinese people?'"

Dr. Hü wrote of the commencement exercises of the class graduating the following year: "Quite a number of the gentry, and the teachers of the government schools for young men, had asked to come to attend the graduating exercises; and of course we were very much pleased to have them. They did seem to enjoy it very much. Some of them have told my friends that they were surprised and delighted to see that their countrywomen could be so brave and do so well. They also wished that their students might have come to see and to listen for themselves. One of the gentry decided that day that his daughter should come to us to study medicine."

Up to this time no girl who did not have a diploma from a mission school had been admitted to the medical course of the Woolston Hospital. But in 1906, yielding to the great desire of many other young women to take medical training, Dr. Hü opened the course to any who could pass an examination on certain subjects which she considered essential prerequisites to a medical course. Four of the seven who presented themselves for examination were passed; only one was a Christian girl, two were daughters-in-law of officials, the other a daughter of one of the gentry.

An extract from the examination paper of one of them shows the real earnestness of purpose with which the work was undertaken. The first question asked was, "Please give your reasons for coming to study medicine?" "Alas, the women of my country are forgotten in the minds of the intellectual world. How could they think of a subject as important as the education of medicine! The result is that many lives are lost, simply on account of no women physicians for women. Though mission hospitals for women and children have been established for a number of years in the Fuhkien province they are far less than we need. For this reason I have a great desire for a medical education, hoping that I may be able to help, and to save my fellow sisters from suffering. It is for this reason I dare to apply for this instruction."

The graduates of the medical course are as yet not great in numbers, but they are doing earnest, efficient work. Some of them have remained in the hospital as assistants or matrons. Of a recent graduating class, one went to the Methodist hospital in Ngu-cheng to assist Dr. Li Bi Cu, the physician in charge; another went to a large village, to be the only physician practising Western medicine; the third to Tientsin, as an assistant in the Imperial Peiyang Woman's Medical College.

V

THE FAVOUR OF THE PEOPLE

As shown by the glimpses of Dr. Hü's work which have been given evangelistic work is carried on in conjunction with the medical work. Christian services are held each morning, and are attended by the dispensary patients, those of the hospital patients who are able to be up, the servants, and usually, also, by a number of visitors. The first year after taking charge of the hospital Dr. Hü was able to report: "Not only some of the in-patients, but also some of our morning dispensary patients, were converted and joined the church on probation. We are rejoicing over the fact that all the hospital servants, all my own servants, and also our teacher, have given their hearts to Christ. They said before a chapel full of patients in one of our morning services, that they would from that day on try to be Christians and to live a good life. So far (six months) they have proved themselves to be in earnest."

A few years later she writes: "In our morning prayers I have often looked and seen a chapel full of people. I have carefully looked over the crowd and I could easily recognize those who have just come to us, others who have been here longer. You wonder how I know it? Well, their faces show. Oftentimes our patients listen so attentively that they forget they are in a crowd. Sometimes one, two, three, or even more, speak up with one voice, 'The Jesus doctrine is truly good. What the leader said is nothing but the truth. Idols are false.'"

In addition to the morning services Christian work is constantly done by the Bible women who work in connection with the hospital. They hold meetings in the hospital wards, teach the hospital patients to read the Bible, do personal work among those waiting their turn in the dispensary, and visit in the homes. One of the missionaries who is a frequent visitor to the hospital says: "No hour of the week brings more fully the joy of service than the hour I spend in the City Hospital with the poor sick folk there. They are always so glad to hear, and so responsive. No wonder the Master loved to heal; and no wonder the Christian physician finds so many open doors."

It is not to be wondered at that those who have been ministered to by this tender, skilful Christian woman, and have watched her happy, busy life poured out in the service of the suffering ones about her, have become convinced that the beautiful doctrine which she teaches and lives is true. Every year the hospital reports contain a record of those who have become Christians during the year as a result of the medical work. Moreover, the seeds sown in the early years of the hospital, some of which seemed to have fallen on rocky ground, were not all in vain. Dr. Hü's sister, reporting the work of 1908, writes: "After careful investigation we found that those seeds were sown deep enough, and with such attention, that even though seven, eight, or nine years have passed they are to-day still germinating, growing, and bearing fruit. After hearing and accepting the gospel, their lives are changed. They become brighter and more straightforward, and have a love for other people."

Christmas is a great event in the Woolston Memorial Hospital, not only for the patients and workers, but also for as many of the neighbours as can be accommodated in the chapel. There is never any difficulty with regard to unwilling guests; on the contrary, the neighbours invariably respond with almost disconcerting enthusiasm. The first year that they were invited to the Christmas exercises, red Chinese cards, reading "Admit one only," were distributed to one hundred and twenty families, one to each house, the choice of the member who should use it being left to the family. Careful explanations as to why all could not be invited were made; but in spite of this, during the days preceding Christmas, the doctor was besieged by the non-elect with requests for invitations.

Dr. Hü's Christmas Party

The guests were invited for half-past seven Christmas evening, but the great majority of them were on hand at four o'clock waiting for the doors to be opened. When they were opened, and the guests began to pass in, presenting their red tickets, a new predicament arose; for it was discovered that many of these tickets were of their own manufacture, the number of those which were passed in far exceeding the number of those which had been given out. But when the doctor looked over the crowds, and saw how eager they were to get in, and how good-natured they were, she had not the heart to turn them away, so told the gatekeepers to let them in as long as they could find a place in which to stand. And although the chapel was crowded to its utmost seating and standing capacity, even the basement and the yard outside being filled, Dr. Hü said that no better behaved or more quiet crowd could have been desired. They listened attentively to the exercises, which were fully two hours long, and at the close, group by group, they all went up to thank the doctor for the pleasure she had provided for them, and then quietly dispersed.

Tea, cakes, and oranges had been provided for the invited guests, but as more than twice the number invited had arrived, it was found necessary to omit that part of the entertainment. However, the doctor sent her servants the following day to distribute the cakes and fruits among those for whom they had been provided. That the guests had enjoyed themselves was evident when the next Christmas drew near, for many either sent to Dr. Hü, or came themselves, to remind her not to forget to invite them to the Christmas entertainment. Nor did a single guest fail to appear on Christmas evening.

If a physician's chief reward is the gratitude and appreciation of those among whom he works, Dr. Hü is indeed rewarded for her self-forgetful service of those whom she lovingly terms "my Chinese." Appreciation of the work she is doing is convincingly shown by the way in which the people flock to her, and in their great eagerness to have the hospital kept open the year around. This has proved to be impossible, although every summer Dr. Hü has made an effort to continue the work, being willing to toil even through the intense heat of July and August, and, since the students must be given a vacation, with only half her usual corps of assistants. One summer she wrote with gratitude that the thermometer in her bedroom registered only 93° that day, after two weeks of 99° and even 100°, and added, "It would do you good if you could see how grateful these people are to see us keeping our hospital open; and we are very glad to be able to do something for them in this very trying hot season."

But the intense heat of a South China summer and the things that it brings with it, make it impossible to keep the work going continuously in the present crowded quarters. Often it is the dreaded plague which necessitates the closing of the hospital doors. One morning Dr. Hü heard that the neighbour directly across the street from the hospital had been stricken with this fatal disease. She closed the hospital at once, and put up a notice telling the patients why it was necessary to close, and assuring them that she would begin work again as soon as it was safe to do so. The next morning the notice had disappeared, and another one which was put up disappeared as promptly. An explanation of this was afforded Dr. Hü, by a remark which she overheard: "How can we stand having this hospital closed? We took the notice down in hope that the hospital would be opened." But when the plague is prevalent, the closing of the hospital is the only safe course to pursue; for one person, coming into the dispensary suffering from this disease, may do more harm in a few minutes than could be undone in many weeks.

A common and gracious way of expressing appreciation in China is the presentation of an honorary tablet, to be set up in one's reception room, on which is written an appreciation of the achievements of the recipient. These are constantly bestowed upon Dr. Hü by those patients who are wealthy enough to express their gratitude in this fashion.

A few years ago fire broke out in the middle of the night not far from the hospital. It burned up to the west wall of the hospital and all along the length of the wall, completely destroying all the houses in front of it. Then it was that the Chinese gave expression in very concrete form to their appreciation of their fellow-countrywoman, and the work which she was doing in that hospital. Dr. Hü says that the building might have been reduced to ashes in a moment had it not been for the faithful efforts of those who "were more willing to have their faces scorched and burned than to leave their work undone," and who laboured to such effect that nothing but the roof was seriously damaged. After the danger was over the people poured in to express their sympathy, and offer their congratulations that the damage was no greater, some of them bringing pots of tea and dishes of food. "This may not seem very wonderful to the people in a Christian country," says Dr. Hü, "but if you knew how the people usually are treated at such times you will agree with me when I say 'Wonderful.'" Fire is usually interpreted as an expression of the displeasure of the gods, and it is considered discreet not to interfere.

Appreciation of Dr. Hü's work is not limited to any one class of people. One day when she was watching the laying of the foundation of her home on Black Rock Hill, many of the people who lived near were gathered around, and she thought it would be a good opportunity to see how they felt about her coming there. So she asked an old "literary man" standing near her, "Ibah, are you glad to see us building? We will soon be your neighbours." Without any hesitation he replied, while the others signified hearty approval of his remarks: "We are all delighted. It is a hospital, and very different from building a church. *I-seng* (doctor), you have made many cures in our families. Of course you don't remember us, but even after the transmigration to either dog or hog we will remember you. You may be sure you are welcomed, only we are not good enough to be your neighbours." After the doctor had left, her chair-bearers told her that the people really meant what they said; for they had heard them say similar things when she was not there. Dr. Hü added, "I do feel very sorry that these people are still ignorant that a mission hospital is a part of the church, but they will know some day."

Nor has appreciation of the work been limited to words. From the magistrates down, the Chinese have readily subscribed gifts of money to the hospital work. Even the Chinese physicians, who have found Dr. Hü's scientific training so formidable a rival to their practice, have exhibited a most friendly spirit. Dr. Hü says of them: "The Chinese doctors have bravely brought their patients for us to heal. Some of them are well-known doctors in the city here, so their coming to us helps our work a good deal. These doctors are not at all conceited. They talk very openly and frankly before everybody."

That Dr. Hü is genuinely loved by her patients, and not valued simply as one from whom benefits are received, was evidenced during her mother's long last illness. During the many months when her mother was so ill, the doctor made the long trip of several miles, from her hospital to her home, almost every night, returning each day for her morning clinics. This, and her care of her mother, added to all her other work, made such heavy days that the patients often said: "Dr. Hü must be very tired. We must save her from working too hard."

This, however, is more easily said than done; for Dr. Hü's sympathetic heart makes it very hard for her to spare herself as long as any one needs her help. For nine years after taking charge of the Woolston Memorial Hospital she worked almost unceasingly, with practically no vacations except those caused by the necessity of closing the hospital in the summer, and these she made as brief as possible. But during all this time the work had been steadily increasing, until finally, in 1907, when the number who thronged the hospital and dispensary was greater than ever before, the doctor's health broke down under the strain, and, although with the greatest reluctance, she was forced to stop work. Her fellow-missionaries insisted that she leave the city during the terrific heat of summer, and go to Sharp Peak for some rest. She had been there only two days when she was taken dangerously ill, and for weeks and months the gravest anxiety was felt concerning her. But she received the best of care and nursing, and finally, in March of the following year, she began gradually to recover.

Some advised that the hospital be closed. But Dr. Hü's younger sister, Hü Seuk Eng, who had received her medical training in the Woolston Memorial Hospital under Dr. Hü King Eng, and had been associated with her sister in the hospital work for some years, said that to close the hospital would be a great shock to Dr. Hü, and a bitter disappointment to the people, and that she would undertake to keep it open. "The load was indeed very heavy and my heart was truly frightened," she admitted afterward. "Every day I just repeated that comforting verse, 'He leadeth me,' and marched forward."

At first the people did not have the confidence in Hü Seuk Eng which they had in Dr. Hü King Eng. Hü Seuk Eng tells of their great eagerness to see her sister: "The faith of many of the patients has been so strong that they thought their illness would at once be cured, or at least lessened, if they could only touch Dr. Hü's garment or hear her voice, or merely look into her face. During these months of sickness many people came wishing to see 'the great Dr. Hü.' They did not want to see me, whom they termed 'the little Dr. Hü.' Some of the leading gentry pleaded with the hospital servants to present their cards to Dr. Hü, and she would be sure to come out to see their sick friends. For it is fully nine years since she was appointed to take charge of this city work, and never once has she been so ill. Indeed, it is the first time she has not been able to respond to pressing calls for medical treatment. So often were heard the words, 'I want the doctor whose hair is dressed on the top of her head and who has graduated from an American college,' that my fellow workers advised the same coiffure in order to avoid trouble; but I told them when the question was asked again just to answer, 'This is Dr. Hü's younger sister, and she will do the best she can.'"

As Dr. Hü grew stronger she was able to consult with her sister as to the hospital work; the nurses and students gave the young physician whole-hearted co-operation; and in time of need Dr. Kinnear, of the American Board, whose hospital is not far away, was always ready to advise and help. Thus the hospital work was successfully carried on under the "Great Dr. Hü's sister, Dr. Hü No. 2," until Dr. Hü King Eng was again able to take charge of it.

As busy as ever, Dr. Hü is back at her work with renewed strength. "I just 'look up and lend a hand,'" she says, in the words of the motto of The King's Daughters' Society of her college. But hundreds and thousands of the suffering ones of her country rise up to call her blessed for the loving, skilful ministry of that hand which has been lent to their needs untiringly for many years, and which they hope will be their strength and comfort for years to come.

That her friends in America recognize the splendid service she is rendering in China, is evidenced by the fact that at its last Commencement her Alma Mater, Ohio Wesleyan University, conferred upon her the honorary degree of Master of Science.

MRS. AHOK

Mrs. Ahok and Her Two Granddaughters

I

THE MISTRESS OF A HOME OF WEALTH

One of the most prominent men in Foochow during the latter half of the last century was Mr. Ahok, a wealthy Chinese merchant. One who had known him for years speaks of him as "a man of remarkable business integrity and generosity of nature." He was very friendly to the Americans and English living in Foochow, and Dr. Baldwin, of the Methodist Mission, was, during all his stay in China, Mr. Ahok's most trusted friend and adviser. Mrs. Baldwin gives a very attractive picture of this Chinese gentleman:

> "When any great calamity through fire or flood came to the people, he was quick to respond with the most liberal aid; and I have known him in times of cholera or epidemic sickness to have thousands of packages of medicine put up by our foreign physicians, for him to give to the sick people. In all our acquaintance with him I never knew him to turn a deaf ear to an appeal for help; in a neighbouring city he supported alone a foundling asylum, in which were one hundred little castaway girls to whom he supplied nurses, clothing, etc., and he assured us that no one besides Mr. Baldwin and myself knew of it. He had for some time been accustomed to come to advise and consult Mr. Baldwin on various matters, and when going away would give him a power of attorney to sign for the firm."

When Mr. Ahok was married, he urged Dr. and Mrs. Baldwin to be present at the ceremony, and gave them the privilege of bringing foreign friends with them if they so desired. His wife was a member of a family of high rank, the sister of a mandarin, and the possessor of an aristocratic little foot two inches and a half long. Outside of those educated in the mission schools, she was the first Chinese woman that Mrs. Baldwin had met who could read and write. One day not long after the wedding, Dr. Baldwin met Mr. Ahok, and disregarding the Chinese custom which makes it a breach of etiquette to inquire after a man's wife, asked about Mrs. Ahok. Mr. Ahok at once answered with evident pride, "She all the same one mandarin; she reads books all the day." He was very proud of her unusual ability, and the confidence and sympathy which soon existed between him and his wife was much greater than is usual in a non-Christian home in China. Mrs. Ahok shared her husband's warm feeling for his foreign friends. The words of Mrs. Baldwin, who knew her intimately, characterize her well:

> "She was, from my first meeting with her, ever a friend of me and mine . . . She was a woman of strong character, of fine personal appearance, always attired in elegant dress, and so perfect in her observance of the elaborate code of Chinese etiquette that it was ever a marvel to me how she remembered the smallest details of the exacting courtesy, never failing to meet the terse and telling instruction of the standard book on etiquette for girls and women, 'As a guest demand nothing, as a hostess exhaust courtesy . . . ' The better I knew her the more I esteemed her."

Mr. Ahok had two beautiful homes in Foochow; one a very fine Chinese house, the other an English residence, elegantly furnished with carpets, pictures, piano, and all other foreign furnishings required for comfort and beauty. In these two homes he and his wife entertained with great hospitality. Mrs. Baldwin says that she has often seen almost the entire foreign community of Foochow, officials, missionaries, and business people, entertained in the Ahoks' home, sometimes in Chinese fashion, sometimes in foreign. It is, of course, contrary to Chinese custom for the mistress of the home to appear before gentlemen outside of her own family. Mrs. Ahok, however, knowing that it was the custom in England and America for the hostess to dispense hospitality to her guests, gradually accustomed herself to appearing as hostess at all gatherings where there were foreign guests; first at small dinners, and later in larger companies. One who was a frequent guest in the home says, "It was a constant surprise to me to see this Chinese lady, so accustomed to seclusion, ever so modestly self-possessed, and in courteous, ladylike bearing, equal to every occasion."

But although ready to conform to foreign custom when entertaining foreign guests in her home, it was several years before Mrs. Ahok was willing to attend similar gatherings in other homes. She frequently called at the home of her friend, Mrs. Baldwin, but never when there were strangers there. On one occasion when Mrs. Baldwin was entertaining a few guests at dinner, she invited Mr. Ahok to dine with them. He accepted readily, and Mrs. Baldwin went on to say: "We very much desire that Mrs. Ahok should come with you. We know your customs, but you have known us for a long time. Cannot Mrs. Ahok make an exception and come on this occasion?" He seemed very much troubled and replied: "I would very greatly like to have my wife come, and she would enjoy doing so, and if there were no one here but Mr. Baldwin and you she would come. But other men will be here, and if she came her chair bearers would know it and her name be injured."

As has been seen, Mr. Ahok was always very friendly to the missionaries and in sympathy with their work. The Anglo-Chinese College of the Methodist Mission, for example, was made possible by his generous gift. But it was some years before he became a Christian. When the step was finally taken, however, he proved to be a most ardent worker, giving generously to the work of several denominations in various parts of China, holding Christian services in his home, and doing earnest personal work among those with whom he came in contact in the transaction of his business, both in Foochow and on his trips to other cities.

Mrs. Ahok was a very devout Buddhist and had no desire at all to learn of Christianity. She was, however, eager to learn English, and consented to learn it through the Bible, since Miss Foster, the English missionary who had been asked to instruct her in English, would consent to give time from her other work only on that condition. "I have often found her with the house full of idols, incense being burned before them," reads a letter from one of her friends. "Our hearts were often discouraged, fearing that this Chinese lady would always love the idols." Even after her husband had become a Christian Mrs. Ahok insisted that she would never forsake the worship of her ancestors and follow the foreign religion. "But," said Mrs. Baldwin, "I felt very sure that a woman of her mind and character would yet follow her husband into the better life. Within a year after, she became a most earnest, loving, working disciple of Christ, ready to deny herself and bear her cross in many ways most trying to a Chinese lady."

Both Mrs. Ahok and her husband had intense opposition to meet, for it was not to be expected that members of families of such high rank should forsake the religion of their fathers without encountering bitter protest from their kindred. The opposition of mother and mother-in-law, both of whom lived in the home with them, was especially hard to bear. Mrs. Ahok's mother was intensely hostile to Christianity, and did everything possible to make things so unpleasant for her daughter that she would renounce her new faith. Mr. Ahok's mother was no less opposed at first; but gradually she became more willing to learn about Christianity, and for some time alternated between her idol worship and the Sunday and mid-week services and family prayers which Mr. Ahok held in his home. At length, after having thus compared the two religions for some time, she announced: "You may take my idol away. Hereafter your God shall be my God." From that time on she was a radiant Christian, and it was not long until Mrs. Ahok's mother followed her example.

At the time of the death of Mr. Ahok's mother, there occurred an interesting example of the way in which a Chinese can become an earnest Christian without becoming less Chinese thereby. In that part of China the wealthy families, and many of those of the middle classes, begin on the seventh day after a death a series of "meritorious" ceremonies for the repose and general benefit of the soul of the departed. In one form or another the ceremonies are repeated every seventh day thereafter until the forty-ninth day. Buddhist or Taoist priests are hired to conduct the ceremonies. Mr. Ahok, probably partly that he might not antagonize his relatives and friends by a disregard of their funeral customs, partly because of the opportunity for spreading the knowledge of Christianity thus afforded, followed the custom of having such a gathering every seventh day. But instead of non-Christian ceremonies being held, the truths of Christianity were preached.

Mrs. Ahok proved to be as active a worker as was her husband. When she had been a Christian only a very short time, the leader for the Friday night meeting held in their home failed to arrive. Evidently her husband was away on one of his business trips, for there was no one else there who could take charge of the service. So Mrs. Ahok said, "I will lead it, though I am not very well instructed in the doctrines of Christianity." In telling of it afterward she said: "I read about the woman who lost the piece of money and took a candle and searched for it; and about the sheep that was lost and found; and then there was singing and prayer; and I spoke to them, and I was able to speak a great deal for them to hear. God helped me and blessed me greatly in the service."

Soon after she had become a Christian she wrote a letter to the Woman's Foreign Missionary Society of the Methodist Church, to be read at their annual meeting. In it she says: "The time for your meeting is so near that thoughts of it are constantly in my heart . . . We have meetings in our *hong* (store), and also meetings in our house every Friday evening. The praise for leading us to know the doctrine, and open the meetings, is all due to the sisters who have not minded that the road to China led them so away from their own country, but have come to teach us of Christianity. Although I do not presume to say that my heart has been deeply sown with gospel seed, yet I know that it has been changed into a different heart . . . Now I send you this letter of greeting, thanking you for your favours, and praising you for your great virtues. May God bless your fervour and spread abroad the doctrine of Christianity in my country. This is what I always pray."

II

WORK AMONG THE WOMEN OF
THE UPPER CLASSES

Interested in every form of Christian service, Mrs. Ahok was especially eager to share the joy of her new-found faith with the women of her own class, the wealthy aristocratic ladies whose secluded lives were so barren and empty, and to whom it was so difficult for a missionary to obtain access. She threw herself with whole-hearted eagerness into the work of the Church of England Zenana Society, whose mission is to these very women, and many are the testimonies to the inestimable value of the work which she did. As one of the missionaries wrote: "She is of immense usefulness in getting the houses open, as she knows the high-class families, and is intensely earnest herself that her fellow-countrywomen should receive the glad news too. Her knowledge of the endless Chinese etiquette and customs, too, is of great service." How difficult it would have been to carry on work of this kind successfully without the help of a Chinese lady of the "four hundred," can be judged from the accounts of the work which the missionaries wrote home from time to time.

Reception Rooms in Chinese Homes of Wealth

"We have paid our first visit to some of the rich families in the city. Mrs. Ahok sent a coolie on the day before to ask if they could see us, and they having signified their willingness, we agreed to meet Mrs. Ahok and go with her. We had some dinner at 12 o'clock, as the city is so far away it takes a great deal of time to go, and then started in our sedan chairs to meet Mrs. Ahok. We found her ready, waiting for us, dressed in a most lovely coral pink jacket, beautifully embroidered, and with very pretty ornaments in her hair . . ."

"After an hour and a half's ride through the narrow, crowded streets of the suburbs we reached the city gates; then through more streets even more thronged, till we reached the house. We were carried through the large outer door, then through a small courtyard, and our chairs put down in a row facing the partition which shut off the next portion of the house. There we had to sit some little time, as I fancy the ladies had not quite finished dressing, but at last out came one of the heads of the family and invited us in. We got out of our chairs and in turn made a sort of low bow to the newcomer, shaking our own hands (Chinese fashion) all the time. This over, she escorted us into an inner room . . . There was a rug on the floor, a round table, some very high chairs with straight backs, and some mirrors. We sat in state some few minutes and then more ladies came in one after another, and each one we had to salute in the same ceremonious way . . ."

"We had to drink tea when we first went in, and later quite a meal was spread on the round table, cakes, fruits, and tea again. We sat at the table with about three of the principal ladies, and the others looked on. I was a good deal struck with the respectful way the young women treat the older ones, always rising when they enter the room, and remaining standing until they are seated . . . We were invited to go and inspect the house, and I was soon quite bewildered at the number of courtyards with rooms all round, which we were led through. I think I was never before in so large a house in China, all one story, but it must cover a great deal of ground. The number of people, too, seemed very great; wives, sons' wives, brothers' wives, children in dozens and scores, servants and slave girls to any number—altogether in that one establishment, one hundred and twenty people."

"At last we finished our tour of inspection, and arrived again in the inner court; but alas! more refreshments were waiting, a bowl of soup for each of us, with some white stuff inside . . . We got through the greater part of the concoction, wiped our mouths with a cloth wrung out in very hot water presented to us by a slave girl, and began to take our leave, bowed to the ladies of the house, begged them to be seated, informed them that we had given them much trouble, but felt grateful for their kindness, and amid repeated requests to 'walk slowly, slowly,' we reached our chairs, alternately calling our thanks, and requests to them to be seated. It is a great thing, going with Mrs. Ahok, for one has a good opportunity of learning many little customs which please them greatly."

"We then proceeded to another house, where we went through much the same etiquette. We were received by a very pleasant old lady and her daughter-in-law, a nice young woman with four dear little children, three of them boys. The old lady is a widow; her husband when living was a mandarin, and her eldest son is now at Peking, preparing to be a mandarin also. We were obliged to drink tea again, and after some time the old lady invited us into her own bedroom, a very much cleaner room than one sees generally, with white matting on the floor and some good furniture.

She was very proud of it, but according to Chinese fashion kept exclaiming that it was such a dirty bad room, that she could hardly ask us into it, but we must excuse it, as it was 'an old woman's room.' We had the concertina brought in again and sang several hymns to which they listened very quietly. One of us read a verse and explained it before singing it, and Mrs. Ahok joined heartily, most bravely acknowledging herself to be a Christian, and telling her friends how happy she was. We then went through the house, and about the middle of the establishment we came on a little enclosure where trees were growing, and a pond of water with a rookery behind it looked quite pretty . . . When we left they begged us to come again, and Mrs. Ahok is so pleased with the reception we received that she is anxious, if possible, to arrange for us to go again next week."

Even more formidable than ceremonious social calls in wealthy Chinese homes, is the thought of entertaining the aristocracy in one's own home.

"I want to tell you about our grand feast," one lady writes. "We had been entertained at several houses, and wished to try to get on more friendly terms with some of the rich city ladies. We feared that they would never be willing to come so far, they so seldom leave their houses for anything. However, through our unfailing friend, Mrs. Ahok, we sent invitations asking them to come and dine with us . . . Sixteen ladies promised to come. The day before, we had to remind them of the day and hour; but according to Chinese etiquette we only sent our cards, and the messenger explained his errand . . ."

"Well, at last the day arrived, and we were busy all the morning making the house look as bright as we could, and getting chairs put about in the verandas and passages. Mrs. Ahok came first, very kindly, and advised us how best to set the tables, etc. She ordered the feast for us, as the Chinese always do, from a shop. So much is paid for a table and everything is provided. Mrs. Ahok lent us all her own pretty things for the table, lovely little silver cups, ornamented silver spoons, red china tea cups with silver stands, and ivory chopsticks mounted with silver; so we were very grand. We had two tables, ten at each. We were twenty in all, counting ourselves."

"At last they began to arrive, and we were kept busy receiving, and conducting them to their seats in the drawing-room. Tea had to be offered at once, and that was hard to manage as none of our men servants might come into the room; so Tuang had to do it all. I do wish you could have peeped in and seen them all sitting about our drawing-room. To us it was a sight that made our hearts dance for joy—and it was a pretty sight too. Some dresses were quite lovely, all the colours of the rainbow, and beautifully embroidered . . ."

"Next on the programme came what the Chinese call '*Tieng sieng*,' fruit and cakes; and during the interval they wandered all over the house examining everything, and we moved about, talking first to one and then to another. Several little things much encouraged us—their friendly, pleasant manner and evident pleasure, and the earnest way in which they pressed us to go again to visit them. One old lady, of a rich mandarin family, said to me in a confidential way, behind her fan: 'Come and see me some day when you have plenty of time, and tell me all about the doctrine, slowly, slowly. I would like to understand about it.'"

"At last the feast was announced, and then came the critical point—seating them at table. One table is supposed to be high, the other low, in point of honour, and at each table the seats are all in order (one, two, three, four, etc.), and it is a mortal offence to give a low seat to one who should be placed high. Mrs. Ahok came to our aid again and pointed out each lady according to her rank and Miss—escorted her to her place. We ourselves had, of course, to take the lowest places."

"Mrs. Ahok then asked a blessing and we began. The principal dish is placed in the centre of the table and the hostess with her own chopsticks helps the guests, all the time urging them to eat, and apologizing for the food, saying she is sorry she has nothing fit for them to eat. Mrs. Ahok did the chief part of these duties for us, and we tried to watch her and do as she did. About two hours we sat at the table, and at last, when we were nearly exhausted, bowls of hot water were brought in, and a cloth wrung out was handed to each person to wash her mouth and hands. The effect on these powdered and painted faces was very funny, but Mrs. Ahok had prepared us for this emergency also, and had sent over her own dressing box—such a beautiful large one—fitted up with everything they could need, powders, paints, and all complete. The ladies were quite charmed and delighted to find such a thing in a foreign house, and adjourned upstairs with great delight to beautify themselves. We heard them telling each other that it was just as if they had been at home . . ."

"At length they said they must go, and we had great leave-taking, bowing and scraping, and thanks, and apologies for having troubled us so much, and assurances on our part that it was all pleasure; and finally off they went, and we sat down to cool ourselves, and drink tea, and chat with Mrs. Ahok. She was very glad and thankful that all went off so well, but quite tired after her exertions, and sat holding her poor little bound feet in her hands, saying they did ache so."

III

A JOURNEY TO ENGLAND

One day when Mrs. Ahok went to call on one of her English friends, Miss Bradshaw, she was startled to find that the physician had ordered her to leave for England on the next steamer, sailing three days later. "I wish you could go with me, Mrs. Ahok," Miss Bradshaw said, when she had told her of the physician's decision. This was a very remarkable suggestion to make to this little Chinese woman, whose life had been such a secluded one that a few years before she would not even accept an invitation to dinner with the Baldwins, since there were to be foreign gentlemen present. Only a short time before, when the Baldwins were returning to America and Mrs. Ahok had gone with them, on her husband's launch, to the steamer anchorage, twelve miles away, they had considered it a great honour, since this Chinese friend had never been so far from home before. But Mrs. Ahok's response was even more remarkable than Miss Bradshaw's proposition; for in three days her little Chinese trunks packed and ticketed, "Dublin, Ireland." Mr. Ahok had heartily consented to his wife's going; and she, unwilling to have her sick friend take the long journey alone, and mindful of the service she might perform for her people in England, by telling of their need and pleading for workers, quickly decided to go.

A letter from a friend who was with her the day she sailed shows the spirit with which she took this remarkable step: "I was impressed with two things; her implicit confidence in her missionary friend, and her sweet, innocent trust in the love and care of her Heavenly Father. She was leaving an elegant home and a large household, and in giving last advice to servants and children her voice was clear and joyous, but I noticed that she often furtively wiped the tears off her cheeks. In her good-bye to her dearly loved aged mother, whose grief was inconsolable, she said: 'Don't grieve, don't worry, just pray and God will take care of me and I will come back. Then we will sit here together and I will have so many things to tell you.' Again and again she said to her children, 'Study your lessons diligently and pray night and morning.'"

Mrs. Ahok sailed from Foochow the 26th of January, 1890. At Hong Kong she was told, "There are a hundred miseries ahead of you," but she answered unflinchingly, "If there were a thousand more I would go." From Singapore she wrote to her husband:

"Yesterday we arrived here at twelve o'clock. Diong Chio (her servant, who accompanied her) wishes very much to go back to Foochow. But I think now I have come so far on the way, I wish very much to obey God's will and go on to England . . . Yesterday we drove in a horse carriage to see Mrs. Cooke. We saw Mrs. Ting's relatives in the school . . . It is very hot here, like Foochow in the sixth moon. I wish you very much to take care of yourself and take care of the children, and do not let them play too much . . . I send *chang angs* (greetings) to the Christian brothers and sisters, so many I cannot name them all, but greet them all. Please sometimes comfort my mother's heart and cheer her that she may be happy in trusting in God all the time. Write to me in Chinese characters, and I can then read it myself; or sometimes, if more convenient, in English, and Miss Bradshaw will read it to me."

A letter from Penang, written two days later, reads:

"Leaving Singapore, a Chinese lady and gentleman came on board our boat to come to their home here in Penang. I saw the lady was very sad . . . so I talked with them, and found they knew your friend in Singapore. I spoke to them of God and the Christian doctrine, and they were very glad to hear. When we arrived here they invited me to their house to breakfast, which was quite a feast. Their house is very beautiful, four stories high. They afterward took me to call on some friends, and then brought me back to the boat on time."

At Colombo she and Miss Bradshaw were met by Miss Bradshaw's sister and brother-in-law, whose home was in that city. Mrs. Ahok wrote from there:

> "We are staying two days and two nights, until our boat starts for England . . . In the evening when it was cool our friends took us to drive, and to call on some Christian people. We saw carriages and horses, so many, running *so* fast; and the roads and streets are *so* wide many carriages can go together on them. We passed many black people; nearly all the people are black. We saw many women and girls with their ears full and covered with ear-rings, and some in their noses too, and some *men* also wear ear-rings. I see the black people, I think how wonderful God's love must be, to give His Son to die for *all the world*, these black people as well as for us. The friends here said they were glad I was going to England to tell the people there about the heathen. They promised all to pray for me, and I want you also to pray that I may fulfil God's will, and do much for God's kingdom in England, and then come back quickly home."

> "It is very hot here, but the evenings and early mornings are cool. Every one goes out to work, or walk, or drive, from daybreak until the sun is hot, and breakfast at ten o'clock. I want to know, when you write, what Heli is doing; and now I am away from home you will take great care of all the children. Please *chang ang* all friends and relatives, and Dr. and Mrs. Sites, and take great care of yourself, that when I return I may find all well. Tell me how the boys are, and don't allow Jimmy to climb the trees. Comfort my mother and tell her all I have written."

Mrs. Ahok was the second Chinese lady of rank to visit England, the first one being the wife of the Chinese ambassador. She was the first Christian Chinese woman England had ever known, and everywhere excited much interest and won warm friends. *The Christian* of London gives an account of a meeting held in the Parochial Hall at Clontarf near Dublin, at which the chairman proposed the following resolution:

"This meeting having assembled to welcome Miss Bradshaw on her return from China; and having learned the extraordinary friendship, tenderness, and devotedness of her Chinese friend, the Honourable Lady of Diong Ahok, mandarin of Foochow, who had at a few hours' notice decided to break through national customs and leave her home and family, rather than allow Miss Bradshaw to undertake the journey alone; hereby records its unbounded admiration of such Christian sympathy, and brave and generous conduct; and they trust that her own and her husband's desire that her visit may excite fresh Christian workers to go to China, may be abundantly fulfilled."

The report of the meeting goes on to say:

"This resolution being carried, Miss Bradshaw intimated to Lady Ahok the purport of what had taken place, and asked her to say a few words of acknowledgment. Accordingly, with the greatest simplicity and self-possession she said (each word of her sentences being translated by Miss Bradshaw) that she was very glad to meet them all, and was very thankful to have been brought to England; that her faith in God had enabled her to come."

The Tenth Annual meeting of the Church of England Zenana Society was held in Princes Hall, London, during Mrs. Ahok's visit to England, and she was one of the principal speakers. In spite of heavy and incessant rain the audience began to assemble before the doors were open. Numbers stood throughout, and many more failed to gain admission. Standing quietly before the large audience, Mrs. Ahok gave her message so effectively that when she sat down, the chairman, Sir Charles N. Aitchison, exclaimed: "Did you ever hear a more simple, more touching appeal under such circumstances? I never did."

Stating the purpose of her visit to England Mrs. Ahok said:

"I have come from China—from Foochow—and come to England for what business and what purpose? The road here was *very* difficult, sitting in a boat for so long! Very tiresome it was, to be on the rough sea, with wind and waves for the first time! My servant Diong Chio and I have come here. We are strangers! We raise our eyes and look on people's faces, but we can see no one we know—no relative, no one like ourselves—all truly strange! I left my little boy, my husband, my mother—all this: for what purpose, do you think? It is only entirely for the sake of Christ's Gospel that I have come."

"It is not for the sake of seeing a new place and new people, or any beautiful thing; we have in China quite close to us new places—beautiful places. I have never seen *them* yet; so why should I come so far to see other places? They may be very good to see, but not for this could I leave my household and people. I cannot speak your words, I do not know any one, and your food is quite different from ours: nothing is at all the same as that to which I am accustomed . . ."

" . . . It was God's Holy Spirit that led me to come. He wanted me to do what? Not to amuse *myself*, but to ask and invite *you* to come to China to tell the doctrine of Christ. How could you know the needs of China without hearing them? How could you hear unless I came to tell you? Now you can know, for I say the harvest in China is *very* great, but the labourers are *so* few. Now my great desire is that the Gospel of Christ may be known on earth as it is in heaven. It is not yet known in China, and because the great houses have not yet heard the Gospel, all their money is spent on the idols, sacrifices, and burning incense."

"In this country *some* help to spread the Gospel, some go to other countries to tell those who have never heard, but some (a great many) are not helping in any way: though they have all heard themselves, they are living here only to obey their own wills, for their own pleasure in this world! How pitiable! We all know the Gospel of Christ; let us then not follow the heathen (who have never heard) in caring for the things of this world. The Bible says, 'If a man receives all the riches of this world, and loses his own soul' (and the souls of many others), 'what can it profit him?' . . ."

"I am only here for a very little, then I must go back to Foochow, where there are so many large houses full of ladies; the workers are so very few now. At this time only one *ku-niong* is there to visit all the great city houses. She is not enough to visit so many; and it is said that in these mandarin houses their ears have never yet heard the doctrine . . . Now I pray God to cause, whether *ku-niongs* (unmarried ladies) or *sing-sang-niongs* (married ladies), *quickly* to go and enter these houses with the Gospel. Now I ask you, raise up hot hearts in yourselves and quickly help us."

"First. Will you come back to China with me?"

"Second. If *you* cannot, will you cause others to come, by sending them and doing what you can to help them to come?"

Mrs. Ahok had planned for a six months' visit in England, but word came that her husband was ill, and she left in July, after a stay of a little less than four months, during which she had addressed large audiences in approximately one hundred meetings in England and Ireland. The impression she had made there may be gathered from a paragraph which appeared in *India's Women and China's Daughters*, after she had left:

> "Those who saw Mrs. Ahok's earnest face, and listened to some of the most simple and heart-stirring words ever heard on an English platform, will recall the impression her plea for her countrywomen then made . . . If God should open the way for Mrs. Ahok again to visit England, she will be welcomed as one who brought home the reality of missions to many a conscience in England, and revived the flagging spirits to zeal for the Lord of Hosts!"

Mrs. Ahok went home by way of Canada, accompanied by Miss Mead, one of the new workers for whom she had been pleading. She did not realize how seriously ill her husband was, for he had written cheerfully: "Tell Mrs. Ahok that I have been a little ill for some weeks and that now I am staying at the Ato house. I find it very restful staying quietly at the old home . . . Tell Mrs. Ahok, please, not to worry at all about me." On saying good-bye to friends in England Mrs. Ahok told them that she hoped to come again, and that the next time it would be with her husband. She was thus spared the keen anxiety throughout the long journey which she must have suffered, had she realized her husband's condition. She wrote back to Miss Bradshaw from Montreal, telling of her safe arrival and expressing her gratitude that although she and her maid had both suffered severely from sea-sickness, they had been well taken care of by "a woman who was a worshipper of God." At Vancouver she had to wait some days for her steamer, and she wrote from there on July 26:

"All well, all peace. From the time I left England a month has passed away. I keep thinking constantly of the meetings in England which we had together. Now we are in this place waiting for the ship and therefore we had this very good opportunity for work. I have been invited by the minister of the church here to speak at meetings. I have done so six times. Because this is a new place, and there are men and women who do not at all believe the Gospel, but who like to hear about Chinese ways and customs, therefore they all greatly wish me to go to these meetings. I think this is also God's leading for us, that we could not proceed on our journey, but must spend this time here . . . To-day is Saturday; this afternoon at half-past three we are to have another meeting; to-morrow we go on board ship to return to China . . . When you have an opportunity, give my greetings to all my Christian friends."

After Mrs. Ahok was back in China, she had a letter from the minister of the Methodist church in Vancouver telling her that three new missionary societies had been formed as a result of her few days' stay. He added, "Your stay here has been an inspiration to us; the fortnight has been one of blessing to us all."

IV

PATIENT IN TRIBULATION

The long anticipated home-coming was a very sad one. During the hot summer months Mr. Ahok had grown steadily weaker, and he died almost three months before his wife reached Foochow. It was a great comfort to those who had been instrumental in arranging for Mrs. Ahok's trip to England to remember how fully her husband had approved of the plan. Miss Bradshaw said: "I shall never forget the bright way in which Mr. Ahok faced all the dangers and difficulties of the journey on which he was sending Mrs. Ahok. As he said good-bye at the anchorage, he said he did it gladly, for the sake of getting more workers for China." Not even when sick and suffering did he regret having let his wife go, although he missed her greatly. He wrote Miss Bradshaw, during his illness, "I realize how great God's grace is, in allowing Mrs. Ahok to visit England, and I am so thankful to all the Christian friends who have helped her and been kind to her."

Mrs. Ahok's brother, her nephew, and Dr. Sites, who had long been a friend of hers and of Mr. Ahok's, met her with a houseboat at the steamer anchorage; and during the twelve-mile ride up the river, the sad news was told. The shock almost stunned Mrs. Ahok at first, but with realization came heart-rending grief. Miss Mead, the young missionary who had come from England with her, wrote soon after their arrival: "Yesterday afternoon I went with three of the ladies to see her. The expression on her face was altered and according to Chinese custom she was very shabbily dressed. Her jewels were taken off. She keeps saying, 'If I could only see him once more and tell him all I have done in England!'"

Added to her grief for her husband, Mrs. Ahok had to bear the taunts and reproaches of her non-Christian relatives, who told her that all this trouble had come as a just punishment of the gods, because she had forsaken the religion of her ancestors, and violated the customs of her country in leaving it for so many months to visit a foreign land. Not only this, but taking advantage of her refusal to perform certain rites of non-Christian worship which are a part of the legal ceremony connected with the inheritance of property, they seized Mr. Ahok's estate, and the dainty little woman who had always been accustomed to every comfort, and even luxury, was left with little but the house in which she lived. Moreover a fresh sorrow followed close upon the first one, as her mother lived only a short time after her return.

But in spite of these heavy burdens, the rare courage which had so often been evidenced before, soon began to reassert itself. Miss Mead was soon able to write: "Mrs. Ahok spoke a little at the Bible-women's meeting on Tuesday, and for the first time came here afterward and had a cup of tea, and saw my room. She is brighter, and I am glad to tell you that she was able to say that the peace of God was still hers. Jimmy Ahok (her little son) was present at Miss Davis' wedding." Nor was Mrs. Ahok too absorbed in her grief to remember her friend in her happiness, for little Jimmy carried with him a beautiful bunch of flowers for the bride.

As soon as the news of Mr. Ahok's death reached England, a letter of sympathy signed by nearly five hundred of Mrs. Ahok's friends in England was sent to her. Its closing paragraph must have brought her comfort in the knowledge that her journey had not been made in vain:

> "We bless God for your coming to England. We have learned to know and love you. Your words are not forgotten. The seed God enabled you to sow is already bearing some fruit, and will, we believe, bring forth much more. One sister has gone with you; we send this by the hands of three more. We know others who were led by your words to offer themselves for Christ's work in China. Two of them are now being trained for the mission field. This will cheer your heart."

To this, Mrs. Ahok replied:

"I thank you all very much for your sympathy, and for sending such good words to comfort me. I rejoiced greatly to hear your words. When I was in England I was a great trouble to you, and I must thank you for all your kindness to me then . . ."

"After leaving England I reached Foochow at the end of the seventh moon, and then heard that my beloved husband had left this world and been called home by God to His kingdom in heaven. At that time I was very sad and distressed, and my distress was the greater because I had no one to carry on our business. Being anxious about money matters, therefore, these many days, I have failed to reply to your letter and to send you my salutations, and thank you all for your great love."

"Now because I cannot carry on trade myself, therefore I have determined to close our business and pay all debts; and the British consul has kindly acted for me in this matter. My hope is that God will enable me to sell this house in which I am living, and then I shall have a competency. It is because I fear that I shall not have enough to feed, clothe, and educate my children that I wish to sell this house. As soon as I have done this I think I shall be able, with the missionary ladies, to visit the houses of the gentry, and have worship with the Chinese ladies, and exhort them all to embrace Christianity. Thus I shall be doing the Lord's work. I trust you will all pray for me, and trust that in some future time an opportunity may be given me of again visiting England and America to work for the Lord. This is the true desire of my heart."

"At this time I seem to have no heart to write, but I send this letter to you to express my thanks. Another day I may write again. My two little children send their greeting, and I add my own. After my return home an additional trouble came upon me because my mother was called home to God. But so far as she is concerned death must be reckoned happiness. She with my husband, earlier than myself, are enjoying the eternal bliss of heaven. I will thank you to give my salutations to all the sisters and ministers whom I know."

Mrs. Ahok soon began again the work among the upper class women which had been her great joy, heartily co-operating with both American and English missionaries in their efforts for these women. Miss Ruth Sites, of the American Methodist Mission, was very eager to do something for the young girls of this class, and Mrs. Ahok gladly lent her influence, with such effect that Miss Sites was enabled to start a small school. Here a good education was given to the daughters of the official class, and Christianity was so taught and lived that by the end of the second year all but two of the pupils were Christians. Miss Sites wrote also of the help that Mrs. Ahok gave in taking her to call in the homes which it would otherwise have been impossible for her to reach.

The Church of England Mission had for some years maintained a school for the daughters of the Chinese Christians in Foochow; but a few years after Mrs. Ahok's return from England they began to feel the urgent need of another school, where girls from non-Christian families could be educated. When Mrs. Ahok's advice was asked, she heartily approved of the plan and advised that it be attempted, offering to rent her home to the Mission for a school building, and promising also to help in the teaching. Moreover she was invaluable in interesting her non-Christian friends in the school, and it rapidly grew from four to forty-five, with such prospects of future prosperity that the house next door to Mrs. Ahok's was also rented, and a new dormitory and dining-room were built.

Girls brought up in non-Christian homes are of course very different from the daughters of Christian parents, and Mrs. Ahok warned the missionaries at the outset that they would be very difficult to manage, and herself drew up the school rules. Her services were of the greatest value, both in this school and in the School for High Class Girls established by the Church of England Zenana Society a few years later, of which she was made the matron. "She makes the girls love her, and her influence over them is good," wrote one of the teachers. "A fortnight ago some money was stolen out of a drawer. I was very sad about it, and the girls were urged to confess, but until yesterday no one spoke. Yesterday Amy told Mrs. Ahok that she had taken it and asked her to tell me." Again she wrote: "Mrs. Ahok makes a very good matron of the school, and an excellent hostess to the many visitors who come to see the school.

Whenever an opening is given Mrs. Ahok and I return the call, and usually get good opportunities of delivering the message."

Testimony is also borne to Mrs. Ahok's effective work among the mothers of the pupils of the school. One of her great joys is a weekly meeting in that wing of the Church Missionary Society's hospital which was erected in memory of her husband, and set aside for the use of women patients.

Throughout her life of whole-hearted service for the women and girls of her country, Mrs. Ahok has been a most devoted mother to her adopted son, Charlie, and her own child, who was always known as Jimmy. The latter inherited his mother's quick mind, and made such a good record at the college which his father's generous gift had founded many years before, that after his graduation he was asked to return as one of the faculty. The beauty of his life was the crowning tribute to his mother. At a meeting held in Foochow, an American, who had recently come there as an insurance agent, told how much impressed he had been by a young Chinese to whom he had been talking, and added that if the Christian schools turned out young men like that, he thought the work was indeed worth while. The young man was Jimmy Ahok.

In the summer of 1904 the young man's wife was very ill, and through the hot summer weeks he cared for her night and day with such devotion that his own health gave out. It was some time before he would admit that he was ill; but he was finally forced to succumb to a severe attack of pneumonia, which ended his life within a very few days. His only anxiety seemed to be that he had not done enough work for his non-Christian neighbours. "I have not tried enough to influence the neighbours," he told his mother. "When I get well I will have a service for them and teach them to worship God." His death was a great blow to his mother, but her work has again been her solace.

One of her friends wrote to England, at the time of her son's death, that the thought that her friends in England would be praying for her was one of the greatest sources of comfort to Mrs. Ahok. In the midst of her busy life in China she has never forgotten England nor her friends there. Some years after her return to China, she sent her greetings to her English friends by one of the returning missionaries, and bade her ask them: "Have you done, and are you doing, all you resolved to do for my sisters in China? So many missionaries have been called home, there can be no lack of *knowledge* now as to the needs of the heathen. With so many to witness to them, how great is the increase of *responsibility* to Christians at home."

She wrote to the women of the Church of England Zenana Society: "You rejoiced to help many ladies to come to Foochow to act as light-bearers and induce those who were sitting in darkness to cast away the false and embrace the true, and to put away all the wicked and evil customs. The work which these ladies are doing is of great value and has helped many. They have preached the gospel in all the region; they have tended the sick in the Mission hospitals; they have opened schools for women and girls in several places, and in my own house. In my own house there are now thirty-nine scholars, some of whom have unbound their feet; and some have been baptized. I myself every week teach in this school, and I also go to the hospital and talk to the sick people. I trust that this seed so widely sown will presently bear fruit, some thirty, some sixty, some a hundred fold. You will remember that when I was in England I told you of the state of things in China; and I hope you will not forget my words but will do your utmost to help China, that God's promised reward may hereafter be yours."

Mrs. Ahok is daily giving herself, in whole-hearted service, to her countrywomen. A fellow-worker has recently written of her:

> "She is winning her way into the hearts of the people in the Manchu settlement. Always bright and cheerful, and ready to tell the Story, she is welcomed wherever she goes. When I think of her past life of ease as the daughter, and later the wife, of an official, I marvel at her spirit of consecration. Quietly she goes from house to house in search of those who are willing to listen. Miles she has walked over the hot stone pavements. 'If my people will only believe in Christ, I shall be well repaid,' she says."

A true Christian woman, whose courage has flinched at no sacrifice, who has borne the loss of husband, mother, son, and property, and the reproaches of non-Christian relatives, with a peace and a faith unshakeable and convincing, Mrs. Ahok is accomplishing much by what she does, doubtless even more by what she is.

DR. IDA KAHN

Dr. Ida Kahn

I

CHILDHOOD IN THREE COUNTRIES

By the time little Ida Kahn first opened her eyes in Kiukiang, China, little girls had become a drug on the market in her family. Her parents had long been eager for a son, but each of the five babies who had come was a daughter, and now this sixth one was a little girl, too. According to Chinese custom, they called in the old blind fortune-teller to declare her fate and give advice concerning her future. His verdict was discouraging for he told them that she must be killed or given away to another family, since as long as she remained in the home the long-desired son would never come to them. The parents were not willing to end the little life, so they determined to engage the baby to a little boy in a neighbouring family, and give her to the family of her betrothed to bring up. But when they called the fortune-teller again to ask his judgment on the proposed betrothal, he declared that the little girl had been born under the dog star, the boy under the cat star, and therefore the betrothal was not to be thought of. The family's perplexity as to what to do with this superfluous little daughter became known to the neighbours, and one of them, who was teaching Chinese to Miss Howe and Miss Hoag of the Methodist Mission, told them about it. That very afternoon they took their sedan chairs and went and got the baby. Thus, when only two months old, Ida was adopted by Miss Howe, whom she always calls "my mother," and of whom she says, "There is no one like her in the world."

The same year that little Ida was born, Miss Howe and Miss Hoag had succeeded in starting a school for girls in Kiukiang, the first girls' school in that part of China. In this school, as soon as she was old enough, Ida began to study. When she was nine years old

Miss Howe went to America and took the little girl with her. They were in San Francisco at this time, and there Ida attended a mission school for the Chinese girls of the city. As most of the other pupils belonged to Cantonese families, and spoke a Chinese dialect very different from that of Kiukiang, she did not learn very much at school; but her stay in America, at the age when it is so easy for children to acquire languages, helped her very much in learning English. On her way back to China Miss Howe stayed in Japan for several months, and there again Ida attended school.

On returning to China, Miss Howe was asked to work in a newly opened station of the Methodist Mission at Chung King, a city of western China, located on the Yangtse River many miles above Kiukiang, and many days' journey into the interior. During their stay there, Ida continued her studies, tutored by Miss Howe and Miss Wheeler, of the same mission. The stay in Chung King lasted only two years, for in 1886 the mission compound was completely destroyed by a mob, and the missionaries had to flee for their lives. For two weeks Ida, with some other Chinese girls, was in hiding in the home of a friendly carpenter, while the missionaries were hidden in the governor's yamen. At the end of that time they all succeeded in making their escape from the city, and the little girl, who had already had so many more experiences in her short life than the average Chinese woman has in threescore years and ten, had the new adventure of a trip of several days through the gorges of the Yangtse River. The river is always dangerous at this point because of the swift rapids, but was so unusually so at that season, when the summer floods were beginning, that only extraordinary pressure would have induced any one to venture on it. The trip to the coast was made in safety, however, and after another stay of a few months in Japan, Miss Howe and her charge went back to Kiukiang, and Ida again entered the school there.

Miss Howe was desirous that the people in America who were interested in the Kiukiang school should be kept informed of its progress; but with her many duties it was difficult for her to find time for frequent letters, so she sometimes asked Ida to write for her. Extracts from one of these letters, written when Ida was fifteen, and sent with no revision at all, show something of this little Chinese girl's acquaintance with English:

"Dear Mrs.—:"

"We have at present twenty-four scholars and four babies. We are not many in numbers, but we hope that we may not prove the works of missionaries in vain. The rules of this school are different from others, since only girls of Christian families are allowed to study. Girls of non-Christian families are allowed to study if they are willing to pay their board. They also furnish their own clothes. For these reasons our school contains girls from many places since Christian girls are few ... In Kiukiang only one Christian family have their girls at this school. The pastor of the church over the river sends his eldest daughter. She has been my companion from babyhood, and we were only separated when she went to Chin Kiang and I to Chung King. She and her sisters never had their feet bound. She is the first girl in Kiukiang who never bound her feet. Her name is Mary Stone. She and I study together both in English and Chinese."

"Her mother came a few weeks ago and stayed with us one week. One day Mary and I went with her to visit the homes of missionaries; when we came back Mrs. Stone suggested that we should go and see her uncle. Mary and I hesitated a little; for we were not used to visiting Chinese homes, especially after New Year when people are very ceremonious. When we arrived at the home we found that they had a New Year's party there, although it was the second month. The reason was this; at the time of the New Year Chinese ladies do not step outside their houses till they are invited to a party, and as invitations do not come until nearly the end of the first month it is common to continue to the second month."

"Mrs. Stone's friends were very glad to see her, for they had not met for a long time. The party consisted of three elderly ladies, besides the hostess, and three young girls besides the young daughter of the house. They were dressed principally in bright blue, green, and red, and were painted to the extreme. The young girls hardly tasted their food, but looked us over from head to foot, especially our feet. The room was hot, and presently one of the

83

girls tittered to another and said, 'Your face is streaked,' meaning that some of her paint was off and showed dark lines; whereupon all the girls declared that they were going to wash their faces. After a while one of the girls came back and said, 'My face is clean now, is it not?' Mrs. Stone told us that they saw we had no paint on and were ashamed of theirs. The girls' only talk was about their jewellry, clothes, and other gossip. Mary and I were very much disappointed, for we hoped to learn some Chinese manners. Mrs. Stone advised me not to wear spectacles, for I attracted many remarks. I told her I was only too glad to draw attention from our feet."

"We always remember the friends in America who for His sake sent missionaries to help us. Yours affectionately,"

"Ida Kahn."

II

AT THE UNIVERSITY OF MICHIGAN

When Miss Howe went to America on furlough in 1892, she took with her five young Chinese people, three boys and two girls; the latter, Ida Kahn and her friend, Mary Stone. Growing up in China, under singularly sheltered and happy conditions, Ida had been greatly impressed with the misery of many of her countrywomen, and early formed the purpose of becoming a physician and giving her life to the alleviation of their sufferings. Mary Stone had the same desire, and Miss Howe, coveting for them a more thorough medical education than was then available in China, took them to Ann Arbor to enter the medical school of the University of Michigan. Both girls passed the entrance examinations successfully, even to the Latin requirements; in fact their papers were among the best of all those handed in.

The four years in Ann Arbor were very busy ones. In addition to their college work, they did their own housekeeping in a little suite of rooms in the home of Mrs. Frost. She says that they excelled many American girls at housekeeping, having regular days for house-cleaning, and always keeping their reception room in good order to receive their girl friends, of whom they had many. Occasionally they even entertained their friends at a little Chinese feast. Mrs. Frost recalls that the only flaw in Ida's housekeeping was that when the girls stopped in her room, as they often did for a little visit on their way home from college, Ida would pick up a book or magazine and become so absorbed in it that she would forget all about the domestic duties awaiting her.

But in spite of college and housekeeping duties, they were not too busy to take part in the Christian work of the church which they attended. Mrs. Frost pays them the following tribute: "They were lovely Christian characters, ready to respond and assist in any Christian work where their services were solicited. While they were in Ann Arbor they assisted me in my Sunday afternoon Mission Band work with the small children of our church, singing, or offering prayer, or telling interesting stories to the little ones. On different occasions they, with the Chinese boys that came with Miss Howe at the same time, assisted me in the public entertainments given to help swell the funds of the Mission Band and raise enough to support an orphan, or for other missionary work. They were very efficient, consecrated Christians, very lovable and loving, highly respected by every one with whom they came in contact. I have very pleasant memories of our little Chinese doctors, and they have a very warm place in my heart and affections."

Both the girls won many friends among both students and faculty. Ida was elected to the secretaryship of her class in her Junior year. Their record for scholarship was so enviable that the assertion was often made, "They must either be remarkably clever, or they must have applied themselves with unusual devotion." They led their class in their Junior year, and in their Senior year were surpassed by only one student. Dr. Breakey, specialist in skin troubles, on whose staff they worked during their Senior year, speaks warmly of their earnestness and devotion to their work. Another professor said at the time of their graduation, "They will be a credit to the University of Michigan. The society which provided for their course will never regret having done so."

As their study at the University drew to a close, the young physicians received many evidences of the appreciation that was felt for the work they had done. Before commencement a reception was given them in the Methodist church of Ann Arbor, at which each of them received a case of valuable surgical instruments. Many other gifts were also showered upon them,—from medical cases, cameras, clocks, and bedquilts, to books and dainty handkerchiefs.

In order not to attract attention they had adopted American dress during their stay in Ann Arbor; but their graduation dresses were sent from China, made in Chinese style, of beautiful Chinese silk, with slippers of the same material,—Ida's blue, Mary's delicate pink. Seven hundred and forty-five students received their diplomas at that commencement, but to none was accorded the universal and prolonged applause which broke forth as the two young Chinese women stepped on the platform to take their diplomas from President Angell's hands. Even the medical faculty applauded heartily, the only time that the staff joined in the demonstrations of the audience. One who was in the audience says, "Their bearing and dignity made us very proud of them." President Angell was much interested in them and said to their friends, "Their future career will be watched with every expectation of eminent success."

The two months succeeding their graduation were spent in Chicago in hospital work, and in the autumn they sailed for China. While they were in America an old gentleman said to Ida, "I am glad you are going back to your country as a physician. Your people need physicians more than they need missionaries." The Chinese reverence for old age was too great to permit Ida to contradict him, but turning to her friends she said quietly, "Time is short— eternity is long." So it was not only as a physician, but as a regularly appointed medical missionary that she returned to China.

III

SEVEN YEARS IN KIUKIANG

Quite a little anxiety was felt concerning the reception which the young physicians would receive from the Chinese on their return to Kiukiang. A foreign-trained Chinese woman physician had never been seen or heard of in that section of China, and, scarcely, in all China, since Dr. Hü King Eng, of Foochow, was the only other in the Empire at that time. The doctors' own friends had long been asking when they were coming back, and when at last the time arrived they had their plans all laid for welcoming them. The missionaries had some doubts as to the propriety of a public ovation to two young women, but the Chinese were so eager for it that they at last consented, and from the moment the young doctors left the steamer until they arrived at the gate of the mission compound, they were saluted with an almost continuous fusillade of fire-crackers. Of course the noise attracted curious crowds, and by the time they reached the Bund they were surrounded by a host of their townspeople who were eager to get a glimpse of the "women doctors." Some of them were heard to say, "Why, these girls are receiving more honour than was shown to our commandant when he arrived!" As the company slowly proceeded up the Bund, the missionaries were besieged with eager questions: "Are they Chinese women?" "Is it true they have been studying for four years in a foreign land?" "Can they heal the sick?" "Will they live in Kiukiang?" When all these questions were answered in the affirmative there was a vigorous nodding of heads, and "*Hao! Hao! Hao!*" (Good, good!) was heard on every side. It seemed remarkable that in so dense a crowd the universal expression of face and voice indicated only favourable interest.

Shortly before the doctors arrived one of the missionaries wrote, "We are expecting 'our doctors' back this fall, and after they have several months of hospital practice in other mission hospitals in China, we hope to have a place ready for them to begin work." The doctors had expected, too, a little time for resting, and visiting with the friends whom they had not seen for so many years. Moreover it was thought that some time would have to elapse before they could gain the confidence of the people sufficiently to begin practice. But on the third day after their arrival four patients appeared and asked for treatment; on the following day the same four returned and six newcomers arrived; and so it went on, until dispensary quarters had to be hurriedly rented and regular work begun.

They had been back only about a month when they were sent for one evening to visit a woman who was in a very serious condition. On arriving at the house they found there the best known native doctor in the city, richly dressed in satin and silk, and accompanied by four chair-bearers. He had told the woman's family that he could do nothing for her, and after welcoming the young women physicians very pleasantly, he took his leave, advising the family to put the patient into their hands, saying, "They have crossed mountains and seas to study about these matters." The family wanted the doctors to guarantee that the woman would live, but they, of course, refused to do this, and after some discussion turned to go. But at that the older members of the family fell on their knees, and begged them to stay and do just whatever they thought best. Their treatment was so successful that three days later the grateful family invited them to a feast, after which they were wound about with red scarfs by the old grandmother, and presented with gifts. The entire family then escorted them home amid the explosion of many fire-crackers.

The *China Medical Missionary Journal* of December, 1896, in commenting upon the work of these young women, says: "They have not, up to the present time, had to endure the pain of losing a patient, although they have had several very serious cases. When that does come, as of course it must, there will doubtless be some reaction, and present faith may be changed to distrust for a time. But the most hopeful had not dreamed of their commencing work without some opposition, and that they actually sought, before making any efforts to secure patients, has been a great surprise to all. Their early success is doubtless due largely to the fact that they are back among their own people as true Chinese, and while they have gained much in culture and intellect, love and sympathy for their race have ever been present; while the ruling motive in all their efforts has been how best to prepare themselves to help their countrywomen. The native women do not stand at a distance to admire them, but familiarly take their hands and feel their clothing; and while acknowledging their superiority do not hesitate to invite them as guests to their humble homes."

Nor was the reputation of the young physicians limited to Kiukiang. At about the time of their return, the young emperor, Kwang-hsi, had issued edicts to the viceroys of the various provinces, ordering them to search out and send to Peking, young men versed in modern affairs, who could act as advisers to him. Several of these young men held a meeting in Nanking before proceeding to Peking. Two of them had heard of the young doctors just returned from America, and, on their way to Nanking, stopped at Kiukiang for the purpose of calling on them. The doctors, however, felt it wise to adopt a conservative attitude in regard to receiving calls from young men, lest their influence with the women with whom they were to work should be weakened, did they violate Chinese custom in this matter. Miss Howe therefore received the guests in their stead, answered their questions, gave them such information as they desired, and presented them with the diploma of one of the doctors. They displayed the diploma at the meeting at Nanking, where it created much interest. The son of Governor Tang of Hupeh, who was at the meeting, spoke for two hours on the desirability of educating women, and suppressing the custom of foot-binding. Then and there a society was organized in which these men pledged themselves to marry their sons only to natural-footed women, and their daughters only into families whose girls were allowed to grow up with natural feet.

At about this time, also, Chang Chih Tung, one of the most eminent and public spirited viceroys of his time, sent a representative to wait upon Miss Howe, with the request that she and the young physicians accept positions in a school which he wished to establish in Shanghai. His aim was to develop a University for women which would train women teachers, and he wished also to have a medical department in connection with it. Foot-binding concubinage, and slavery were dealt with directly in the prospectus; Sunday was to be observed as a holiday; and liberty of conscience in the matter of religion was to be allowed. While no religious books might be taught in the school, no objections were raised to religious work being done privately. When this request was brought to the Women's Conference of the Methodist Mission they passed a resolution expressing their sympathy with the proposed plan, and advising the acceptance of the positions by Miss Howe and one of the doctors, "if in the process of the development of the plans they feel it best to do so." Although as the plans developed Miss Howe and the doctors finally decided that they could be more useful in Kiukiang, the offer shows the interest felt in the work of the young physicians, even in the highest official circles.

At the close of the first year, Dr. Kahn reported:

"With the exception of a month spent at the Nanking Memorial Hospital we have kept up our work steadily ever since our return to Kiukiang. At present we have regular dispensary work, and our Bible woman spends her time faithfully teaching the women. As she is quite an elderly woman, has been very well trained and educated, and above all is an earnest Christian, we are sure that her influence will not be small on those with whom she is brought in contact. Then again, she is a good chaperon to our girls who are preparing to be nurses. There are three girls who have been in the girls' school from five to six years, and now choose to take up nursing as their life work. They assist in the dispensary, help make up the drugs, attend to the hospital patients, and recite two lessons to us every day. Later on we hope to have them assist in our operations and go out with us when we need them."

"At present we have six patients in the hospital, and although the number may seem small, yet our hospital has been opened scarcely two months, and it is so tiny that it appears quite full. The hospital is merely a Chinese dwelling, heightened and improved by floors and windows."

"During the year two or three interesting trips have been made by us into the country. The first one was made by Miss Stanton and myself to the capital of the province, to attend the wife of an official. We brought her home with us, and while here undergoing treatment she studied the Bible every day and enjoyed it very much. Later, when she returned home, she recovered completely, and now two of her sons are in our mission school. Her husband gave one hundred dollars for the dispensary and two merit boards or tablets to us, and he said he would help us in raising money for the hospital . . ."

"One thing which pleases us very much is that those whom we have treated outside, when they get well almost invariably come and call on us, and even go with us to church."

The following year she wrote:

"The time has come again for us to give our yearly report and we are very glad to be able to say that the work has advanced in every direction. The year has been a very unhealthy one and fevers have simply flourished, so that our nurses have been kept very busy caring for patients often in a critical condition. During the year we were enabled to make four visits into the country. Miss Stanton has been more free to do evangelistic work and take long trips than previously, and it has been a privilege for one of us doctors to accompany her on the journeys. By taking turns, one of us could always attend to the regular work. People are awakening everywhere, and crowds flock to us to hear the truth and receive medical treatment. Sometimes we dispense medicine to one or two hundred people a day. Our stock of medicine usually gives out, and many people have had to be turned away for lack of drugs. Everywhere they begged us to come and visit them again. At one place a party of women came at night to the boat where Miss Stanton and I were staying, inviting us to go ashore and organize a church. They told us: 'Men can hear preaching sometimes on the street; but we women never have an opportunity to hear anything except when you ladies come to teach us.'"

During that year, the second of their practice, the young physicians were able to report 90 patients treated in the hospital,

134 in homes, 3,973 in the dispensary, and 1,249 during country trips, making a total of 5,446.

Their third year was also a very prosperous one, not only in their work among the poor, but also in the number of calls which they received from the class of people who were able to give them ample compensation for their services. This money was always turned into the mission treasury by the young physicians, who also, for four years, gave their services to the Woman's Missionary Society without salary, in return for the four years of training which they had received at Ann Arbor. An interesting glimpse of the impression they made upon their fellow-workers is given by a letter from one of the missionaries written at this time: "None who know our beloved doctors, Mary Stone and Ida Kahn, can do otherwise than thank God for raising up such efficient and faithful workers. It is difficult to think of any desirable quality which these two ladies do not possess. To this their growing work gives witness."

Dr. Kahn was honoured in the latter part of the year by being appointed as the representative of the women of China to the World's Congress held in London, June, 1899.

The hearts of the doctors were gladdened during this year by the prospect of a hospital building in which to carry on their work. Early in 1900 Dr. Kahn wrote happily to Dr. Danforth, whose gifts had made the building possible:

> "Work on the building is going on merrily, and the results are pleasing so far . . . As to our work at present, we can truly say that never before has it seemed so encouraging. This being the Chinese New Year month we have usually had scarcely any patients, and at least for a number of days no patients at all; but this year we had no day without patients, and often had thirty, forty, and even over fifty patients a day, which is certainly unprecedented. You cannot imagine how strong a prejudice the average Chinaman has against doing work of any kind too soon after New Year's. Not only is it the only holiday of any duration they have during the year, but it is ill luck to work too early."

> "While standing at the gate on the second day, watching the patients straggling in, I saw one of them brought on a stretcher. It was a pretty little girl who had been badly

burned by the upsetting of a foot stove under her wadded garments. As they came up an old woman who carried one corner of the bamboo bed called out, 'Doctor, have you opened your accounts yet?' meaning have you begun work yet. I answered, 'Why, our accounts have never been closed, so we did not need to reopen them!' 'Yes,' she said, 'I know, and I wish you many congratulations for the New Year, and may you have much custom during the year.' Think of what that implies! Then she went on volubly describing what a time they had in getting people to carry the bed, for no money could induce them to come, and finally she and a few boy cousins had to bring her. A few days ago her people came and fired lots of crackers, as well as hung up long strips of red cloth outside our gate, in order to show people that we have accomplished a cure for them and they wish to express their gratitude in public."

A few months later the Elizabeth Skelton Danforth Memorial Hospital was completed; but just as they were about to occupy the new building the Boxer uprising assumed such serious proportions that all work had to be dropped, and the women were forced to leave the city. The doctors accompanied the other missionaries to Japan, and remained there for a few months; then came back to China and spent a few weeks in Shanghai, until the country had quieted down sufficiently to make it safe to return to the interior. The weeks in Shanghai were not idle ones, for they found plenty of patients to treat during their stay there.

There were many missionaries from various parts of China gathered in Shanghai at this time, and the women improved the opportunity thus afforded by the presence of so many workers for a conference on the various phases of women's work. Dr. Kahn was asked to give an address on Girl Slavery at this conference, and made a great impression by her powerful plea for the abolition of this wicked practice. Her appeal had added force because she was a Chinese woman herself, and this evil custom had come close to her life. "She was my best friend in school," she said of one victim, "and her mind was as beautiful as her person. We were baptized together and she confessed to me that she would like to devote her life to Christian work, adding so sadly that she must try first to help her opium-smoking father. Where were gone her longings and aspirations when she was sold by him to be the concubine of a man sixty years of age! Surely on this eve of China's regeneration, we, the more favoured ones, must plead with all our might that all these unnatural customs shall be swept away with the last relics of our country's barbarism."

A Nurse in Dr. Kahn's Hospital

The doctors were soon able to recommence work in Kiukiang, and with their fine new hospital they worked under far more favourable conditions than heretofore. A letter from Dr. Kahn tells of their enjoyment of the new building: "It is now a pleasure to see the little crowds of women and children sitting comfortably in the easy seats of the dispensary waiting room, and to notice how they enjoy the talks of the Bible woman. In former years they were always huddled together in a dark room, or else were scattered here and there in our front yard, and the Bible woman had great difficulty to get them to listen quietly. The new drug room is a constant delight. The operating room, too, is our pride, because it is so light. The confidence which people had in our work before last year's troubles broke out, appears to revive again."

The following summer, Miss Robinson, of Chinkiang, visited the doctors in their new quarters. A letter written from their home reads: "We find them as skilful in housekeeping as in hospital-keeping, and excelling in the happy art of making their guests at home. Such all-round women are a priceless boon to their native sisters. I want to have our graduates attend the coming annual meeting in Kiukiang, improving this opportunity of bringing them in contact with the doctors, who have long since become the ideals of our school girls . . . Referring to the fear some native Christians have shown of sending their girls to a school having manual labour in its curriculum, Dr. Ida exclaimed hotly, 'This fear of work is the bane of China.' Here are two doctors of exalted privileges, educated abroad, honoured alike by native and foreigner, and yet putting their hand to cooking and housework of every kind, as the need may be, without a thought of being degraded thereby; a glorious object-lesson to accompany the teachings of the mission schools."

IV

PIONEER WORK IN NANCHANG

In the first year of the young physicians' practice in China, a launch had been sent to Kiukiang by one of the high officials of Nanchang, the capital of Kiangsi province, with the request that one of the physicians should return to Nanchang in it and treat his wife, who was very ill. Dr. Kahn went, and brought the woman back to Kiukiang with her. After a few weeks under the doctors' care she returned to Nanchang completely recovered, and gave such glowing accounts of the benefit she had received that many of the wealthy ladies of the city followed her example and went to the Kiukiang hospital for treatment.

At that time no American missionary work was being done in Nanchang; but the successful treatment of the wife of the official is said to have "opened the gates to Protestant missionaries." The Methodist Mission soon established a station there, and the work grew rapidly in spite of the fact that Nanchang was not an altogether easy place in which to work. As it was in the interior and off the highway of travel, little was known of foreigners. Moreover, there was a rowdyish element of the population which was very hostile to them and everything connected with them, as Dr. Kahn had good cause to know. Soon after the work in Nanchang had been begun by their mission, she and Miss Stanton made a trip there, the latter to do evangelistic work, Dr. Kahn for medical work. Dr. Kahn shall tell the story of their experiences:

A Village Crowd

One of Dr. Kahn's Guests

"One afternoon, Miss Stanton and myself went to call on some ladies of the Plymouth Brethren Mission, the only other Christian mission besides our own in the city. The day being warm Miss Stanton had the rain cover of her sedan chair removed. Unfortunately it was a hired chair and there were no side curtains, neither was there an upper curtain in front. When we had gotten fairly started boys began to follow us, and by the time we had reached our destination quite a crowd was with us, and rushed into the compound ahead of us. Once in, we planned to cover the chair; and also waited till dark for our return, hoping that by that time the crowd would have dispersed."

"However, when we got ready to start, there was a large crowd still clustered around the court and door. They allowed Miss Stanton to get into her chair first and start off, but when I followed, then the fun began. The coolies would take a step or two, then the chair would be pulled almost down. Yelling at them was of no avail. Finally a stone was thrown and one of the windows broken, so I thought it was time to walk. The crowd called out, 'A foreigner! a foreigner!' I was almost ready to cry with vexation, and could not help telling the people that they were cowards and barbarians. One or two of the bystanders now began to take my part, and administered a blow or two to those who seemed to be too obstreperous, telling me at the same time not to be afraid. I started to enter the largest residence near me, but the gatekeeper slammed the door in my face so I went on ahead. One of my volunteer helpers said, 'There is the residence of the official Yang, where you can find shelter.' So he led me into a house where a couple of women were sitting in the great room. Rather abruptly I told them that I was pursued by a crowd, and asked if I could find shelter there until I could send word to my people. My guides also explained that the people took me to be a foreigner. To my surprise the ladies welcomed me cordially, and ordered the doors to be shut on the crowd. Now all my friends will be ashamed to know that I could not repress my tears, but after a good cry I felt relieved. The people in the house urged me not to be afraid. I told them I was not afraid; I was disgusted that my people could be so mean. My hostess related several instances where ladies coming home alone in their chairs had been pulled about, and deplored the fact that there were so many rowdies everywhere."

"Very soon the church members heard of my trouble and came to escort me home. As we wended our way homeward fresh members joined us till we formed quite a procession with lights flashing everywhere. Indignation was felt by all, so some of the party went back to demand the arrest of the ringleaders. How thankful I was to get back safely to our mission compound. Miss Stanton's chair coolies had assured her that I was following behind, and she thought everything was secure. The church members were at prayer meeting and did not notice my non-arrival. The delay I think must have been providential, for had the members rushed there and found a crowd, I fear more trouble must have resulted."

"Very soon the husband of a wealthy patient came and offered many apologies for the bad conduct of the people. How do you suppose he found out about the matter? He was returning home from a feast, and seeing so many Methodist lanterns (please do not smile, for the lanterns have 'Methodist Church' written on one side, and 'Gospel Hall' on the other) asked what it meant, and learned of the trouble . . . Certainly the devious ways of my own countrymen never struck me so forcibly before. How much we do need the truth to shine in upon us and change us completely."

Yet it was to this city that the Christian physician's heart went out in such compassion that, for its sake, she was not only willing, but glad to leave her home in Kiukiang, the prosperous work which she had been doing in fellowship with her lifelong friend, Dr. Stone, and the beautiful new hospital to which she had long looked forward with so much eagerness.

"This old city of Nanchang with about three hundred thousand inhabitants, and surrounded by a thickly settled country, has not a single educated physician," one of her letters reads. "Do you know what that means? The people realize their need and asked us to go and live among them. One of the church members offered to give us, free of charge, a piece of land situated in a fine part of the city, for either a hospital or a school lot. The pastor said he could raise $1,000 among the people if we would only begin medical work there. Do you think we ought to refuse that offer, which is a wonderful one, because the church has only just been established there? 'And when they came to Jesus they besought Him instantly, saying that he was worthy for whom He should do this.'"

The people of Nanchang, both Christian and non-Christian, pleaded so eagerly for medical work, and promised to do so much toward its support, that the missionaries agreed with Dr. Kahn in feeling that a door to great opportunity was open before her, which it would be a serious mistake not to enter. Accordingly, early in 1903, she responded to what Dr. Stone termed "the Macedonian call," and began work in Nanchang.

The Woman's Foreign Missionary Society did not feel able to assume any responsibility for the financial support of the medical work in the new field, beyond that of the doctor's salary. But Dr. Kahn firmly believed that missionary work should be just as nearly self-supporting as possible; and since many of the urgent invitations from Nanchang had come from homes of wealth, she was very willing to attempt to carry on medical work there on a self-supporting basis. In an article on the subject of self-supporting medical missionary work, written for the *China Medical Missionary Journal*, she gave some of her reasons for believing in self-support, and her theories as to how it might be carried out.

> "To the many of us, no doubt, the thought naturally arises that we have enough problems to deal with in our work without having to take up the irksome question of self-support. Yet at the present time, when every strenuous effort is being made to evangelize the world in this generation, any plan which can help forward such a movement at once assumes an aspect of vital importance in our eyes. Let it not be presumed that self-support is to be recommended as possible to every medical missionary. On the contrary, I fear, only by those fortunate enough to be located in large cities could the effort be attempted with any hope of success. Yet in a measure the question concerns every one of us, because in its different phases self-support is sure to be pressed upon all of us with more or less force. Personally, my work was undertaken in Nanchang partly from faith in the principle, partly because there were no funds available to institute medical work on any other basis. My faith in the principle is founded upon the belief that anything of value is more appreciated when something has been asked in exchange for its worth, from those perfectly able to effect the exchange . . . The ordinary people who

seek help from the missionary will retain a higher measure of self-respect, and also suspect less the motives of the benefactor. The rich will appreciate more highly the services received, besides having the added glow of satisfaction in helping forward a worthy charity . . ."

"There should be no ironclad rules, however; each case must be counted on its own merits. Generally speaking, it might be well for the physician in charge to state plainly that the very poor are to be treated free of charge and have medicines, and occasionally food supplies, gratis. Those a little better off may help a little in paying for the medicines. The next step above that is to pay partly for the treatment as well; while the highest grade is to pay in proportion to the amount of help received. All this means a good deal of thought on the part of the physician and assistant, but gradually it will become routine work and so demand less labour."

"Is self-supporting work a missionary work? Assuredly yes; for is not the money thus gained used in giving relief to the poor? . . . And if all money received goes again into the work, to increase its efficiency, why may it not be counted missionary? Part of it is given as thank-offering by those who are not Christian, and all is given for value received from Christian effort. Our Lord healed diseases without money and without price. If we ask, 'What would Jesus do?' under our existing circumstances, the suggestion comes to my mind that it would be something different in form, but not in principle, from what He did in a different land, under far different circumstances, nineteen hundred and more years ago. Someone says we are to follow Jesus, not to copy Him; and the principal thing, it seems to me, would be always to abide in the Spirit of the Christ, by whatever method we feel constrained to render our little service."

Although the new step was taken so bravely, it was not an easy one. Some idea of the courage it required is shown by the doctor's report of her first year in Nanchang; "The very thought of making a report causes many poignant memories to rush upon us. With what hesitancy and timidity did we begin our work in the new field!

Knowing our own limitations, it was not with a light heart that we began the new year. Yet," she was able to add, "as we toiled on, we could but acknowledge that we were wonderfully led along 'The Pathway of Faith.'"

Enough money was contributed by the Nanchang people to enable Dr. Kahn to rent a house in the centre of the city, in which dispensary work could be carried on, and in which she lived. They also supplied her with a small stock of drugs with which to begin work, and she treated something over two thousand patients during the first eight months. The number seemed small after the work to which she had been accustomed in Kiukiang; but she was becoming known in the city, and in addition to her patients several of the women of the city had called on her in a purely social way, many of them educated women of the official class. Dr. Kahn says of them:

> "As the wives and daughters of expectant officials they are representative of the better class of the whole country, for they are assembled from every province. It is pleasing to note that dignity and modesty are often combined with real accomplishment among them. It is amongst these that there is a marked eagerness to learn something better. They talk about their country incessantly, and deplore with real sincerity her present condition, of which many of them have a fairly good knowledge. To these we tell over and over again that the only hope of China's regeneration is in her becoming a Christian nation, and that only the love of Christ can bring out the best qualities of any people . . ."

As to the financial side of the work, Dr. Kahn reported: "The outlook is most promising. During the eight months I have received over $700 from the work, and as much more has been subscribed."

During the succeeding two years the work developed steadily. The number of patients treated at the close of 1905 was almost three times the number reported in 1903, and Dr. Kahn wrote, "We have tried to check the number of patients, simply because we did not feel financially able to treat so many." The rent which she had been obliged to pay for her building in the city had been a heavy burden financially. Great was her delight therefore to be able to report, at the end of this year, a new $2,000 building for dispensary purposes, the money for which had been secured partly from fees, partly from subscriptions. "With the incubus of a heavy rent off our shoulders we may be able to relieve more patients, as we would wish," she wrote.

The dispensary building was not the sole cause for rejoicing that year; for in addition to it a fine, centrally located piece of land, worth $3,600, was given for a hospital site. "All the assistance received has been from the gentry and not the officials, and therefore it really represents the people and we feel much encouraged by the fact," reads Dr. Kahn's report. The gentry wanted to make over the deeds of the property to the doctor. This, however, she would not permit, but insisted that they be made in the name of the Woman's Foreign Missionary Society of the Methodist Church, assuring the donors that the work would then be on a permanent basis, as it could not be if the deeds were made out in her name.

It would not have been just cause for discouragement had the work dropped off the next year; for a dispute between some French Catholic priests and the Nanchang magistrates led to such serious disturbances and bloodshed that the missionaries were obliged to flee for their lives. Dr. Kahn refused to leave her work until the last possible moment, and returned just as soon as it was at all safe to do so. At the end of the year she was able to report that although it had been necessary to close the dispensary for three months, fully as many patients had been treated in the nine months as in the twelve months of the year previous. Another gift had also been received from the gentry, a piece of land near the hospital site, on which a home for the physician was already in process of building.

During 1907 the work continued to grow steadily in scope and favour. Dr. Kahn's annual report for that year shows something of its development: "My practice has increased steadily among the foreigners and Chinese, until now we have patients come to us from all the large interior cities, even to the borders of Fuhkien. You would be surprised to know how many foreigners I treat in this out-of-the-way place. During the year we have treated over eight thousand patients. The evangelistic work among them has been better undertaken than ever before, and I am sure we shall see results in the near future. Several inquirers have been accepted, and seven women have been taken in as probationers."

Although the demands of her work in Nanchang are constant and absorbing, Dr. Kahn has never become provincial in her interest; while working with whole-hearted devotion in her own corner, she still keeps the needs of the entire field in mind. At the fifth triennial meeting of the Educational Association of China, held in Shanghai in the spring of 1905, she gave an address on "Medical Education," in which she said in part:

"Turn the mind for a moment to the contemplation of China's four hundred millions, with the view of inaugurating effectual modern medical practice in their midst. How many physicians are there to minister to this vast mass of humanity? Barely two hundred! Such a ratio makes the clientele of each physician about two million. What would the English-speaking world think if there were only one physician available for the cities of New York and Brooklyn! Yet the people of these cities would not be so badly off, because of the steam and electrical connections at their command."

"We as missionary physicians recognize our own inadequacy and the imperative demand for native schools. How can we undertake to help spread medical education in China with the limited means at our command? Shall we simply take unto ourselves a few students as assistants, and after training them for a few years turn them out as doctors? By all means, no! Take us as we are generally situated, one or two workers in charge of a large hospital or dispensary, is not the stress of our professional work almost as much as we can bear? Then there are the people to whom we ought to give the bread of life as diligently as we minister to their bodily needs. Add to this the urgent need of keeping up a little study. Where comes the time and strength to teach the students as they should be taught? Certainly to the average missionary such work as the turning out of full-fledged doctors ought to be debarred. It seems to me that what can and ought to be done is to single out promising students who possess good Christian characters as well as physical and mental abilities, and send them to large centres such as

Peking, Canton, Shanghai, and Hankow, where they might take a thorough course in medicine and surgery. In these large cities the case is altered; for hospitals and physicians are comparatively numerous, and much could be done in a union effort. I am glad one or two such schools have been inaugurated."

"As stiff a course as possible ought to be arranged and if it is thought best the whole thing might be outlined by the China Medical Missionary Association. For entrance requirements there should be presented a solid amount of Chinese and English, with some Latin and perhaps one other modern language. That may seem a great deal to ask at present, but our higher schools of learning ought soon to be able to supply such a demand, as well as the necessary training in mathematics, physics, chemistry, etc. In other words the student must be equipped in the very best manner for his lifework."

"During the present generation at least, if not longer, the women of China will continue to seek medical advice from women physicians, and to meet the demand we must confront and solve another problem. Co-education is impracticable just at this juncture. We must have either an annex to the men's college, or a separate one entirely. Whichever plan is adopted it matters not, barring the 'lest we forget' that it is just as important to establish medical schools for women as for men."

"In the golden future when schools abound we shall have to think of state examinations; but at that time we shall expect to be ready to greet the blaze of day in this wonderful country of ours, when she has wakened from the long sleep we often hear about, and taken her place among the nations of the world, and God and man shall see 'that it is good.'"

At the close of 1907 Dr. Kahn had been back in China for twelve years, years of arduous, almost unremitting labour; and her fellow missionaries felt that before the work on the new hospital building began she ought to have a vacation. Certainly she had earned it. Not only had she worked faithfully for seven years in Kiukiang, but she had, within the five succeeding years, established medical work in a large city, where she was the first and only physician trained in Western sciences. Assisted only by two nurses whom she herself had trained, she had kept her dispensary running the year around, all day and every day. Moreover, she had kept the work practically self-supporting, in spite of the fact that she had refused to economize by using inferior medicines, or bottles of rough glass which could not be thoroughly cleansed. She had insisted that her drugs be of the purest, and dispensed in clean, carefully labelled bottles, and had often furnished besides the food needed to build up strength. In addition to all this, she so commended herself and her work to the people of the city that in 1906 she was enabled to hand over to the Woman's Foreign Missionary Society, a dispensary building and two fine building lots, to be used for a hospital and physician's home.

She was finally persuaded to go to America for a period of change and rest. "Rest" for Dr. Kahn evidently means a change of work; for she went at once to Northwestern University to take the literary course which she felt would fit her for broader usefulness among her countrywomen. Eager to get back to China she did three years' work in two, studying in the summer quarter at the University of Chicago, when Northwestern closed its doors for the vacation. In addition to her University studies, she undertook, for the sake of her loved country, a work which is peculiarly hard for her, and almost every Sunday found her at some church, telling of the present unprecedented opportunities in China.

The question may perhaps be raised as to whether days could be crowded so full and yet work be done thoroughly. But Prof. J. Scott Clark of Northwestern University said of her, at this time: "Dr. Kahn is one of the most accurate and effective students in a class of eighty-four members, most of them sophomores, although the class includes many seniors. The subject is the study of the style and diction of prominent prose authors, with some theme work. Last year Miss Kahn attained a very high rank in the study of the principles of good English style during the first semester, and in that of synonyms during the second semester. In the latter difficult subject she ranked among the very best students in a class of over three hundred members. She is very accurate, very earnest, and very quick to catch an idea. In fact she is nothing less than an inspiration to her classmates."

In the spring of 1910 Dr. Kahn was a delegate to the Conference of the World's Young Women's Christian Association held in Berlin, and from there went to London for six months of study in the School of Tropical Diseases. She had planned to return to Northwestern University to complete the work interrupted by her trip to Europe, and to receive her degree. Her work had been of so unusually high a standard, however, that she was permitted to finish her course by correspondence, and was granted her degree in January, 1911. She completed her course in the School of Tropical Diseases with high honour, and in February, 1911, she reached Nanchang, where one of her fellow-workers declares, "she is magnificent from the officials' houses to the mud huts."

The new hospital was still in process of building, but the doctor began work at once in her old dispensary, and the news of her return soon spread. In a short time she was having an average of sixty patients a day, and several operations were booked some time before the hospital could be opened. It was ready for use in the autumn and in October Dr. Kahn wrote: "The work has gone on well, and patients have come to us even from distant cities clear on the other side of Poyang Lake. The new building is such a comfort. It looks nice and is really so well adapted for the work. I would be the happiest person possible if I did not have to worry about drug bills, etc . . . It is impossible to drag any more money out of the poor people. Our rich patients are very small in number when compared with the poor. Yesterday I had to refuse medicines to several people, though my heart ached at having to do so. You see I had no idea that the work would develop so fast, and things have risen in prices very much the last few years."

At the time that this letter was written the Revolution was in progress, and Nanchang, with all the rest of Central China, was in a turmoil. Because of the disturbed conditions most of the missionaries left the city, but Dr. Kahn refused to leave her work. With the help of her nurses she kept the hospital open, giving a refuge to many sufferers from famine and flood, and caring for the wounded soldiers. None of the forty beds was ever empty, and many had to be turned away.

The close of the Revolution did not, however, bring a cessation of work for the doctor. She already needs larger hospital accommodation, three times as much as she now has, one of her friends writes. But Dr. Kahn delights in all the opportunities for work that are crowding upon her; for she says, "When I think what my life might have been, and what, through God's grace, it is, I think there is nothing that God has given me that I would not gladly use in His service."

DR. MARY STONE

{Handwritten} Yours in His service
Mary Stone

I

WITH UNBOUND FEET

On the "first day of the third moon" of the year 1873, a young Chinese father knelt by the side of his wife and, with her, reverently consecrated to the service of the Divine Father the little daughter who had that day been given them. They named her "Maiyü,"—"Beautiful Gem"—and together agreed that this perfect gift should never be marred by the binding of the little feet. It was unheard of! Even the servant women of Kiukiang would have been ashamed to venture outside the door with unbound feet, and the very beggar women hobbled about on stumps of three and four inches in length. No little girl who was not a slave had ever been known to grow up with natural feet before, in all Central or West China. That the descendant of one of the proudest and most aristocratic families of China, whose genealogical records run back without a break for a period of two thousand years, little Shih Maiyü, should be the first to thus violate the century-old customs of her ancestors, was almost unbelievable.

Even the missionaries could not credit it, not even Miss Howe, whose interest in the family was peculiarly keen, since Maiyü's mother was the first fruits of her work for Chinese women, and had ever since been working with her. To be sure Mrs. Shih had said to her, "If the Lord gives me a little daughter I shall not bind her feet." But Miss Howe had made so many efforts to induce the women and girls with whom she had worked to take off the crippling bandages, without having been successful in a single instance, that she did not build her hopes on this. One day, when calling in the home and seeing little Maiyü, then five years old, playing about the room, she remarked, "My dear Mrs. Shih, you will not make a good job of it unless you begin at once to bind little Maiyü's feet." But Mrs. Shih never faltered in the purpose which she and her husband had formed at the little girl's birth, and promptly answered, "Did I not tell you I should not bind her feet?"

The first years of Maiyü's life were unusually happy ones. Her father was a pastor in the Methodist church, and had charge of the "Converting to Holiness" chapel in Kiukiang; her mother was successfully conducting a day school for girls. From her mother Maiyü received much of her earliest instruction and before she was eight years old she had studied several of the Chinese classics and memorized the Gospel of Matthew and the catechism in Chinese so thoroughly that she has never forgotten them.

But as she approached the age when custom required that her feet should be bound, the little girl discovered that the way of the pioneer is not an easy one. The unbound feet were a constant source of comment and ridicule, not only by older people, but by other children as well. She was stopped on her way to school one day by an older girl, who taunted her with her "big feet" and refused to let her pass unless she would kneel down and render obeisance to her own bandaged stumps. The small descendant of the proud house of Shih absolutely refused to submit to such humiliation; but it was only after her mother's assistance had been invoked that she was allowed to proceed on her way.

Relatives and friends protested vigorously against such apparent indifference to their daughter's future on the part of her parents. "You will never be able to get a mother-in-law for her," they declared. Mr. and Mrs. Shih felt, no doubt, that this was true; for who could have then prophesied that the time would so soon come in conservative old China when young men would not only be willing to marry girls with natural feet, but would decidedly prefer them! Maiyü's father and mother never reconsidered their decision that their daughter should grow to womanhood with natural feet; but they did try to devise some plan by which her life might be a useful and happy one, even though she might never enjoy the blessing of a mother-in-law. They were very much impressed with the service which Dr. Kate Bushnell was rendering the suffering women and children of Kiukiang, and when Maiyü was eight years old her father took her to Dr. Bushnell and announced, "Here is my little girl. I want you to make a doctor of her."

This was almost as startling as the unbound feet! A Chinese woman physician was unknown and undreamed of. But this young father's faith in the possibilities of Chinese womanhood was not to be discouraged. The necessity of general education, preliminary to medical training, was explained, and Maiyü was put in charge of Miss Howe, then at the head of the Girls' Boarding School of the Methodist Mission. In this school she spent most of the next ten years of her life, studying in both Chinese and English, and fitting herself under Miss Howe's direction for her medical course.

In 1892, Maiyü and her friend, Ida Kahn, accompanied Miss Howe to America, there to receive the medical education for which they had long been preparing. If America held much that was new and interesting to them, it was no less true that they were something new and very interesting to America. "What makes these girls look so different from the other Chinese women who come here?" the Government official who examined their passports asked Miss Howe. "All the difference between a heathen and a Christian," was her prompt response.

That there were Chinese girls who could successfully pass the entrance examinations to the medical department of the University of Michigan, in arithmetic, algebra, rhetoric, general and United States history, physics, and Latin, was a revelation to the people of America, and their college career was watched with the greatest interest.

While in Ann Arbor, Maiyü took pity on the professors who found it so difficult to pronounce her Chinese name, and decided to use the English translation of it, Mary Stone, during her stay in America. Accordingly one morning when the professor started to call on her, she announced, "I have decided to change my name, professor." The burst of laughter with which the class greeted this simple statement was most bewildering to her; but after she had seen the joke she often declared that she was "one of the products of Christianity, an old maid," for, as she pointed out, an unmarried woman is practically unknown among non-Christians.

During her medical course Mary became more strongly impressed than ever before with the evils of foot-binding. Her mother's feet had, of course, been bound in childhood, and although Mrs. Stone had never bound the feet of any of her daughters, she had not unbandaged her own. For she said that if she also had unbound feet people would say: "Oh, yes, she must be from some out-of-the-way place where the women do not bind their feet, and so she does not know how to bind the feet of her daughters. That accounts for such gross neglect." On the other hand, she reasoned that if she herself had the aristocratic "golden lily" feet, it would be evident that her failure to bind her daughters' feet was due to principle. But while Mary was pursuing her medical studies she became convinced that the time had come when her mother ought to register a further protest against the harmful custom, by unbandaging her own feet, and wrote urging her to do so. Mrs. Stone readily agreed to this. Moreover, at the annual meeting of the Central China Mission in 1894, when a large mass-meeting was held for the discussion of foot-binding, she ascended the platform and in a clear voice, which made every word distinctly heard to the remotest corner of the large chapel hall, told why she had never before unbound her feet, and why she was now about to do so. Her husband was so in sympathy with her decision that later in the meeting he added a few words of approval of the course she had taken. The last shoes worn before the unbinding, and the first after it, were sent to Ann Arbor to the daughter who had so long been a living exponent of the doctrine of natural feet.

After four years at the University of Michigan, during which she and her friend, Dr. Ida Kahn, had won the respect and friendship of both faculty and students by their thorough work, Dr. Stone went to Chicago for the summer, in order to attend the clinical work in the hospitals there. It was at this time that she met Dr. I. N. Danforth of that city, who was ever afterward her staunch friend. He was about to leave for Europe, but found time before his departure to introduce Dr. Stone to many of the Chicago physicians and hospitals. He says: "She won the hearts of all with her charming ways, and got everything she wanted. When I took her to clinics she would often not be able to see at first, being such a little woman; but the first thing I knew she would be right down by the operating table. The doctors would always notice her, and seeing that she couldn't see would open up and let her down to the front." After what Dr. Danforth considered a thorough clinical training, including visits to practically all the good hospitals in Chicago, Dr. Stone sailed for China with Dr. Kahn, reaching there in the autumn of 1896.

II

THE DANFORTH MEMORIAL HOSPITAL

On their return to China, Dr. Stone and Dr. Kahn received a most enthusiastic welcome from the Chinese. It had been expected that it would be necessary for them to spend the first few months in overcoming prejudices and gradually building up confidence. But on the contrary, patients appeared the third day after their arrival, and kept coming in increasing numbers, until in December it became necessary to rent dispensary quarters and rebuild a Chinese house to serve as a hospital. Dr. Stone reported in July, 1897, that since October of the preceding year, she and Dr. Kahn had treated 2,352 dispensary patients, made 343 visits, and had thirteen patients in their little hospital, besides spending a month in Nanking visiting the hospitals there.

The following year the little hospital was presented with what was probably its first, though by no means its last, "merit board." One of Dr. Stone's letters gives an account of this event:

"Two days ago we had quite an occasion. A child had been sick for a long time, and the best Chinese physicians pronounced him incurable. Then it was that they gave us a chance. He is recovering and the parents, wanting to show their gratitude, gave us a 'merit board,' thinking in this way they would 'spread our fame.' Accordingly a day was selected to present the board to us, and we prepared tea and cakes for those who would come. On the day appointed at 2 P.M., we heard a lot of fire-crackers, rockets, and guns, and a band playing the flute and bugle at the same time. The 'merit board,' consisting of a black board with four big carved and gilded characters in the centre, and with red cloth over it, was carried into our guest hall by four men, and set on the centre table. The characters complimented us by a comparison with two noted women of ancient times, who were great scholars. I acknowledged the honour with a low Chinese bow, and a tall, elderly gentleman returned me a bow, without a word being spoken by either of us. Then I withdrew, and he took tea with two of our gentlemen teachers. The company stayed to see the board put up on our wall."

As the fame of the young physicians grew and their practice steadily increased, they found themselves greatly hampered by lack of a proper building in which to carry on their work. In 1898 Dr. Stone wrote back to America: "Our tiny hospital is crammed full. An observer might think that we carried home but a slight idea of hygiene. Our hospital measures on the outside 28 by 21 at Chinese feet (our foot is one inch longer than yours) and we have been compelled to crowd in twenty-one sleepers. The building being so small and not protected from the heat of the sun by any trees or awnings, by evenings it is fairly an oven, which is certainly not a very desirable place for sick people. We are looking forward all the time for signs or signals from the women of America to build our new hospital, but not a letter comes to bring us this kind of message. Still we are thankful for the hope of building some time."

This hope was realized almost at once, largely through the generosity of the friend Dr. Stone had made in Chicago, Dr. I. N. Danforth, who felt that no more fitting memorial could be erected to his wife than a hospital for Chinese women and children. Dr. Stone and Dr. Kahn drew their own plans and sent them to Chicago, where they were perfected in every detail by an architect of that city, and sent back to Kiukiang with the necessary specifications and instructions. These plans were carried out to the letter and in 1900 an airy, grey brick building, finished with white granite and limestone, plentifully supplied with comfortable verandas, and bearing over its pillared entrance the name, "Elizabeth Skelton Danforth Memorial Hospital," was ready for occupancy. But on the very day that the furniture was moved in, the American consul advised all foreign women and children to leave Kiukiang immediately. The other missionaries were so unwilling to leave the young doctors to face the possible dangers from the Boxers alone, that they finally prevailed upon them to go to Japan with them.

The hospital escaped any injury, however, and in her report for 1900, Dr. Stone said: "Our new hospital is a comfort and constant inspiration to us in our work. We were indeed grateful, after half a year's enforced exile, to come home and find it intact and ready for use . . . During six months there have been 3,679 dispensary patients, 59 in-patients, and 414 visits."

Elizabeth Skelton Danforth Memorial Hospital,
Kiukiang, China

The hospital was formally opened on the seventh of December, 1901, during the annual meeting of the Central China Methodist Mission, held that year at Kiukiang. The *North China Daily Herald* gives the following account of this interesting occasion:

THE OPENING OF A MODEL HOSPITAL IN KIUKIANG

"On Saturday afternoon the 7th instant, some foreign residents of Kiukiang, the members of the Methodist Central China Mission, and many native friends gathered together at the formal opening of the Elizabeth Skelton Danforth Memorial Hospital, of which two ladies, Drs. Stone and Kahn, are the physicians in charge. There were a number of Chinese ladies, whose rich costumes showed the official rank and wealth of husbands and fathers. The Chen-tai, prefect, assistant prefect and magistrate added their official dignity to the occasion. These were noticeably appreciative of the first hymn, 'God save the Emperor.'"

"Bishop Moore presided, formally opening the hospital; Mr. Clennell, H.B.M., Consul for Kiukiang, gave a very good address, to which Dr. Stuart, American Vice-consul of Nanking, made fitting response. Then followed short, pithy speeches by Drs. Beebee and Hart. The two heroines of the occasion kept modestly in the background, refusing to be introduced, much to the disappointment of the audience. The officials insisted that coming forward would be in entire harmony with etiquette and propriety, but the Chinese young ladies remained firm and were represented by their wise teacher, Miss Howe, who has planned with them and for them since their childhood. After refreshments guests were at liberty to saunter across verandas and through the various wards, the room for foreign patients, the convalescents' room, solarium, dark room, offices, reception room, etc., of this admirably planned hospital. The operating room with its skylight, its operating table of glass and enamel; the adjoining sterilizing room, containing apparatus for distilling, sterilizing, etc., are especially interesting to Chinese visitors. The drug rooms are well stocked and furnished with modern appliances, instruments, a fine microscope, battery, etc., and there is the nucleus of an excellent library. Everywhere one finds evidence of wise forethought and careful expenditure."

Dr. Stone, Dr. Kahn, and Five of the Hospital Nurses

"The Chinese have a high regard for the skill and ability of these gifted young physicians. One sees this appreciation, not only in the commendatory tablets hanging in the entrance hall, but in their equally gracious and more serviceable gifts, which together with fees amounted this year to about $2,500. The doctors have had within the last twelve months, 7,854 patients and have made 531 out-visits. Their services have been requested by different official families of Kiukiang and Nan-chang, the capital of Kiangsi. Patients come to them from different provinces. The young physicians fearlessly make journeys far out in the surrounding country, crossing the mountains perhaps, but always in perfect safety, as they meet only with respect and courtesy. Sometimes after a successful visit their chairs will be draped with a red cloth and the physicians will be carried home in triumph through an admiring crowd,

121

and accompanied all the way by fire-crackers. They hear only pleasant and complimentary remarks from passersby. 'We are afraid of foreigners, but you can understand our nature'—so the simple-minded country folk sometimes tell them."

Dr. Stone, describing the opening of the hospital to Dr. Danforth, wrote, "The Chinese were very much impressed with your way of commemorating your wife." Dr. Kahn added that one of the highest officials, who was being shown through the building, signified his approval by emphatically declaring, "It would make any one well merely to stay in such a pleasant place."

As a matter of fact, work had been carried on in the new building for some time before the formal opening. It had been ready for occupancy none too soon, for in the summer of 1901, the Yangtse River overflowed its banks, working great havoc among the crops and homes of the people living near it. Dr. Stone wrote Dr. Danforth: "Tens of thousands have been rendered homeless and destitute. Some of them are literally starved to death. The sick and hungry flock to our gates, and for several months we have had over a thousand visits each month to our dispensary." Some idea of the part which the hospital played in relieving the sufferings of the flood refugees is given by an article in *Woman's Work in the Far East*, written by Dr. Stone at about this time:

> "Perhaps friends would like to know how we dispensed the clothes and quilts so kindly sent us. During the winter months very many needy refugees came to our dispensary daily for treatment. Of course we did not have enough clothes to distribute indiscriminately, but only for those who were the most helpless and miserable. We received them by hundreds, and not only had we to give out medicine, but rice, as well as clothing."
>
> "One morning when it was raining outside, an old woman came into our dispensary all exhausted, carrying a child on her back, and another buttoned in front within her clothes. The older one was a boy three years old and the tiny baby in her bosom was only three months old. They proved to be her grandchildren, and the old woman said:

'Never in our lives have we gone out to beg before, and for the last three days we have not had a morsel to eat. Before the floods we were considered well-to-do people, and my son is forty years old and a literary man; so he is too ashamed to beg, but tries to help the family by gathering sticks for the fire. His wife is sick in bed with typhoid fever and now the baby has no one to nurse it, and the boy is sick, and I have to take care of them all and beg for a living.' The woman had on only a lined garment, so we gave her one of those wadded gowns that were sent us, and a tin of milk for the baby, and also sent a little rice to make gruel for the sick woman at home."

This was only one of many cases of need which the hospital sought to alleviate. A few days after Christmas of this year Dr. Stone wrote to a friend in America: "What a busy time we had getting ready to celebrate the joyful event! We gave a good square meal to the refugees, and let them take home what they could not finish here. It made me feel happy to see them so pleased, and gave us an opportunity to tell them of the greatest Gift to mankind. Although we were so rushed that we did not even sit together to eat our regular meals, yet we felt it was the happiest Christmas we have ever had."

In addition to the refugees larger numbers of regular patients than ever before were coming to the doctors for treatment. The new hospital had hardly been opened before Miss Howe wrote, "Patients who are able to bear their own expenses are being sent away, because the present accommodations are already overtaxed."

Just at this time, when the doctors' growing reputation, and the increased facilities which the new buildings afforded, were greatly enlarging both opportunity and responsibility, the question of Dr. Kahn's going to Nanchang to open medical work there arose. It is not surprising that at first Dr. Stone wondered how she could spare her friend and fellow-worker, now that the work was greater than ever before, and every indication pointed to large growth in the future. But when she became convinced that the opportunity at Nanchang was too great to be neglected, and that only Dr. Kahn could meet it, she bade her God-speed and cheerfully accepted the added burden thus laid upon her.

Left alone with the entire work in Kiukiang, Dr. Stone's hands were full indeed, as the answer which she gave to a request for a synopsis of her day's work shows: "We breakfast at half-past seven and then I go to the chapel in the hospital and conduct prayers for the inmates and patients able to attend. After prayers I make a general inspection of the hospital, and then I teach my class of nurses. I take young native girls in their teens and give them a thorough course of training such as they would get in America. I translate the English books into Chinese for them, and sometimes put the Chinese books into English too. Then I go to the dispensary and am busy there for hours ... In the afternoons I make calls, generally on women of rank who need my assistance and have been unable to get to the hospital. I return home only when here seems no further work for me that day."

So far from decreasing in number after the medical force had been lessened by half, the stream of patients became larger than ever. A few weeks after Dr. Kahn had gone, Dr. Stone said, in a letter to Dr. Danforth: "For a long time I have been wanting to write to you, but have been so pressed with work that I had to let my correspondence suffer. Now I find that I must write to you to let you know how crowded we are already, at this season when we generally have a scarcity of patients, as it is Chinese New Year. Now that our work is better known we seem to draw a better class of people. I don't mean very rich people, but the well-to-do, thrifty class, who earn their way by labour. Just now I have to accommodate seven private patients who are paying their own way, with only two private rooms at my disposal. So what do you think I do? I had to put one in our linen room, one in the sewing room, one in a bathroom, and finally, as a last resort, we had to put one in the nurses' dining-room ... We generally have to put patients on the floor in summer, but I am afraid we will not have enough room to accommodate more even on the floor."

Dr. Stone's dispensary patients soon averaged a thousand a month, and as the people's confidence grew, her surgical work also became much heavier. In 1906 she reported: "In looking over the record for the year we realize that we have advanced decidedly in gaining confidence with the people. *Tai-tais* (ladies of rank) who formerly refused operations, returned to us for help."

Often her work kept her busy far into the night and she not infrequently fell asleep from sheer exhaustion as she was carried home, in her sedan chair, from some difficult case in the country. Yet her work was well done. The tribute of a fellow-missionary was well deserved: "Dr. Stone is a tower of strength in herself and with her trained assistants carries the large work here nobly. She has been eminently successful in surgical cases and is having more and more to do in this line." Another, working in a different station, wrote, "It was my happy fortune to be the guest of another ideal Chinese woman, Dr. Mary Stone, at Kiukiang. I saw her in her model hospital, where every little wheel of the complicated machinery was adjusted to perfect nicety."

As the work grew, it became evident that larger accommodations would soon be imperative, and Dr. Stone succeeded in securing some additional land. The first addition was a lot which she had long desired to enclose within the hospital grounds. For some time she was unable to do this because of a road which ran between, but in 1905 the road was moved to the other side of the lot, at her petition, and the land was included within the hospital compound. "Most of the neighbours have been patients and are friendly," one of her letters reports. "When the magistrate came to see about moving the road to the other side of the lot only one man objected. He was soon pacified by the magistrate's remark that 'the hospital here is for the public good, and when it is in our power to do it a service, we should gladly do it.'" Another piece of land was purchased during the same year, by money raised entirely from the Chinese.

The next addition greatly delighted Dr. Stone's heart. Adjoining the hospital was a temple known as "The White Horse Temple." This was so close to the hospital that it made one of the wards on that side damp and dark, and, moreover, the noisy crowds of people who thronged it, and the beating of the temple gongs, made it a most undesirable neighbour for a hospital. Immediately after the annual meeting at which Dr. Stone had been enabled to report the purchase of the other lots, a cablegram came from America with the good news that $1,000 had been secured for the purchase of the temple and the lot on which it stood. Purchasing a temple is quite sure not to be an easy task, but in spite of many hindrances Dr. Stone succeeded in securing the lot and in making what she gleefully termed "a real Methodist conversion" of the temple into an isolation ward.

In 1896 Dr. Stone had landed in China and with Dr. Kahn begun medical work in a small, rented Chinese building. In 1906 she found herself in sole charge of a large, finely equipped hospital for women and children, with a practice which was increasing so rapidly as to make constant additions to the hospital property necessary.

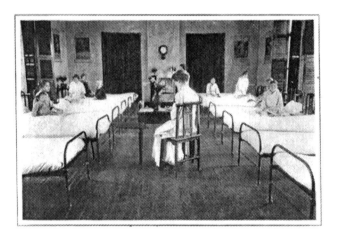

General Ward of the Danforth Memorial Hospital

III

WINNING FRIENDS IN AMERICA

In 1907, after eleven years of almost unceasing labour, during four of which she had carried the growing work at Kiukiang entirely alone, except for the help of the nurses whom she herself had trained, Dr. Stone reluctantly laid down her beloved work for a few months. During the winter of 1906 she had a severe attack of illness which she herself diagnosed as appendicitis, and for which she directed treatment which brought her relief. But renewed attacks finally convinced her and her friends that she must submit to an operation if her life was to be saved. It was decided that she should go to an American hospital, for as a fellow physician located at another station of the mission wrote, "We all have a very high regard for her and her work, and wanted her to get the best that could be had." Moreover, it was a good opportunity to get her "away from China for a much-needed change and rest."

Accordingly Dr. Stone, accompanied by her friend, Miss Hughes of the Kiukiang mission, sailed from Shanghai, February 9. President Roosevelt, who was acquainted with her work and knew of her serious condition, had a telegram sent to the Commissioner of Immigration at San Francisco, giving instructions that the Chinese physician be admitted with no delay or nerve strain. She was therefore passed at once, with all consideration and all possible help.

From San Francisco Dr. Stone went straight to the Wesleyan Hospital in Chicago, that she might be under Dr. Danforth's care. The operation was entirely successful, and early in April, less than a month after reaching America, she was sufficiently recovered to take the trip to Miss Hughes' home in New Jersey, where she was to rest for a few weeks.

Complete rest, however, was an impossibility to Dr. Stone, even during her convalescence, so long as there was any service she could render. Two weeks after her arrival Miss Hughes wrote Dr. Danforth that "our little doctor" was accompanying her to several of the meetings which she was addressing, and was "making friends right and left for her work." Boxes of instruments, pillows, and spreads for the hospital beds, a baby organ for the hospital, the support of a nurse, and other useful things were being promised by these new friends. "Her smiling face, with no word from her even, is a wonderful revelation to people who judge the Chinese by the putty-faced laundrymen, the only specimen of China they have ever seen," said Miss Hughes. Dr. Stone spent the month of May in New York, attending lectures and clinics in the hospitals there. As she was starting for Chicago at the end of May, she wrote Dr. Danforth:

> "Do you think I shall be able to see much clinic in two weeks? That is the only time allotted me, and my only hope is that you will be the 'master of the situation,' and help me to spend every minute to the best advantage . . . I have attended as much clinic as I possibly could this month, but it is awfully hard to get around in New York. Do you suppose I would be able to go directly to Wesley Hospital Monday, and do you think Dr. J—would have the time and the interest to show me the inside methods of the hospital? He wrote me a most kind letter and invited me to do so . . . Two weeks will mean a lot if I can be right in the inside track of things. I want some time on the eye and ear work, besides a few clinics on dermatology. I know two weeks will not be enough for the much I want to see and know, but since it is the only time I am to have, I know you will help me to make the most of it."

Thus did the indefatigable little doctor take the "much-needed rest" of which her friends in China had written. That she did make the most of her two weeks is testified to by Mrs. Danforth, who visited many of the hospitals with her, and who says: "In visiting the hospitals she never missed a thing. She saw everything—nothing escaped her notice, not even the laundries. She was always keenly alert for every idea that would improve her hospital."

On her way back to the East, Dr. Stone stopped at Ann Arbor, for she was eager to revisit her "dear old campus," and the faculty under whom she had taken her medical work. "We had a lovely time in Ann Arbor," she said in writing to a friend. "Dr. Breakey, in whose home we stayed, arranged a meeting, or reception, where I saw most of my old professors. Then in the parsonage we met all the ladies of our church. Next day I had a meeting in the church."

The next few months were filled with almost incessant labour, chiefly speaking and making friends for her work. The cordial responses which she met everywhere never became an old story to Dr. Stone and her letters are full of enthusiastic accounts of them. "Here at Silver Bay, a society wants to support a missionary and we hope to find the missionary to-night. The first was yesterday's work and the second we hope to gain to-day." Again, "Last night on the car we met a gentleman whom I know through my sister Anna, and after a few minutes' talk he wants to give me his camera, 5x7, for hospital work. Isn't that splendid?" Or, "This morning we went into a flower-seed store and what do you suppose the proprietor did but to give us the seeds, a big list of all kinds we wanted, and then offered to add a few more varieties. We are having lots of fun here."

Dr. Stone met with no less enthusiasm in public meetings than in her contact with individuals. One of her hostesses tells of her remarkable success in arousing genuine interest in her work: "She spoke at churches very often while she was with us, and not once did she fail to get what she asked for. She did not ask for things in general but for definite things,—pillows for the beds, lamps for the gateway, etc. She is irresistible."

The same friend tells of the glee with which Dr. Stone, whose English is perfect, delighted to learn modern slang phrases. After practising them in the bosom of the family she would sometimes innocently introduce them into her addresses, invariably bringing down the house thereby. At one meeting, after telling a most remarkable story, she remarked, "You may think this is a whopper, but it is true!"

Reports of the meetings at which she spoke contain such items as this: "The pastor of St. James Church offered to duplicate all money given in the collection when Miss Hughes and Dr. Stone spoke. Six hundred and eighty-two dollars was the result. A gentleman present offered one hundred dollars for a speech from Dr. Stone in his church. The speech was made and one hundred and eighty-two dollars put in the treasury." Other items read: "At the district meeting a new auxiliary came into being in—Church. No one could resist Dr. Mary Stone's persuasive tones as she went up and down the aisles asking, 'Won't you join?' She told the people how much she needed a pump in Kiukiang and forthwith the pump materialized." The *New York Herald* gave a long and enthusiastic report of her work, ending with the words: "'Am I not fortunate? And I am so grateful to be able to help a little!' is the modest way she sums up a work of magnitude sufficient to keep a corps of medical men busily employed."

Everywhere this little Chinese woman made friends. The words of one of her hostesses are emphatic: "She was in our home for a month, and she is one of the most attractive women of any race I have ever met. She is so charming that she wins her way everywhere." "She is so gracious and cordial," said another. "She came into our family just as a member of it. I was not very well at the time and she gave me massage every night. Her whole life and her whole interest is in doing for others. And the wonderful thing about her is her ability to do so much." "No missionary that we have is more greatly loved," is the verdict of another.

Dr. Stone greatly enjoyed her stay in America. "Dr. Danforth called my appendix 'that blamed thing,'" she said. "I call it that blessed thing, because it brought me to this country and people have been so kind to me." But she was eager to return to Kiukiang, and early in September was on her way back to China, rejoicing in renewed health and new friends for her work, and in the many gifts which were going to make that work more efficient.

IV

A VERSATILE WOMAN

Chief among the gifts which Dr. Stone received for her work while in America, was the entire sum of money needed to build another wing to the hospital. The need of this wing had been felt for years, for the hospital had become crowded as soon as it was opened. Dr. Stone's ingenuity had been taxed to the utmost to enlarge the capacity of the original buildings, by putting patients into rooms designed for far different purposes, and even partitioning off sections of the halls for them. Still many whom she longed to take in had to be turned away. Many times it had seemed as if the much-needed addition were almost a reality. But the money would not be quite sufficient; or the contractors could not be secured; or prices of building material would rise and the cost would prove to be double that originally estimated; it seemed as if the wing were too elusive ever to materialize. On her return to Kiukiang work on the new wing was commenced, and it was finished the following autumn. This addition practically doubled the hospital work, and Miss Hughes wrote that Dr. Stone was in "the seventh or seventeenth heaven over it all."

At the same time that the new wing was being built, a little bungalow was erected in the hills behind the city, where children with fevers could be sent to escape the intense heat of the summer months in Kiukiang. "The Rawling Bungalow is finished and the children are all up there for the summer," Dr. Stone wrote in 1908. "I know you will be delighted at this annex to the hospital. Of course it is only a bungalow . . . but it is a blessed relief to have this place to which to send the sick little ones and those who otherwise would be left to suffer here all summer."

As soon as the masons had finished their work on the new wing of the hospital they began on another new building just beside it; a home for the doctor and Miss Hughes, also a gift from friends in America. That, too, was completed by the end of 1908, and during Chinese New Year, a time when the hospital work was less pressing, Dr. Stone and Miss Hughes took a trip to Shanghai to buy furniture for it. It is easy for one who saw the doctor then to imagine the keenness with which she noticed every detail in the American hospitals, for while visiting in the homes of friends in Shanghai nothing escaped her quick eye. Miss Hughes' attention was constantly called to things that pleased the doctor's taste by her often reiterated, "Look here! We must have this in our home." "Miss Hughes and I shall try to make our home so homey," she wrote to a friend, "and we shall open it for everybody, the everyday, common folks as well as the *Tai-tais*."

The next addition to the hospital property was a home for the nurses, money for which had been pledged during Dr. Stone's stay in America. As soon as the funds were sent out building was commenced, and in March, 1909, the nurses moved into their new home. The accommodations of the hospital were thus enlarged still further, and moreover the nurses had a far more restful environment in which to spend the hours when they were off duty.

Nurses of the Danforth Memorial Hospital

One who met Dr. Stone in America spoke of the great impression made upon her by the doctor's ability to do many things. The demands upon the physician in entire charge of the large Danforth Memorial Hospital are indeed many and varied, but Dr. Stone has proved equal to them all.

She is a good general practitioner. Probably the best proof of this is the number of patients who throng the hospital gates. In 1908 she reported, "Last month we saw over 1,700 people in the hospital and dispensary, and in April we saw over 1,800." A year later she wrote, "Taking the statistics for last month I found we treated 2,743 in the month of April." Her successful treatment of the most difficult diseases is all the more remarkable to one who knows the tendency of many Chinese not to consult a physician until the patient is at the point of death. Their utter lack of knowledge of the simplest rules for the care of the sick, and the dreadful surroundings in which so many of them live, produce, in those who are brought to the doctor after long weeks of suffering, conditions which are almost too terrible to describe.

The words of a fellow-missionary throw light on the difficult character of Dr. Stone's work:

> "Talk of missionary work! People at home don't know the meaning of the word! Here is this plucky little woman in the midst of this awful heat—I dare not go outside of a shaded room until after the sun is down at night—treating anywhere from twenty to fifty patients in the dispensary every day, and her charity ward filled with the most trying, difficult, repulsive cases of suffering humanity. Missionary work? Why you don't even *find* such cases as she has every day, in the hospitals of America. How the people live as long as they do—how these poor little suffering children survive until they get to the state they are in when brought to the hospital, is more than I can understand."

Dr. Edward C. Perkins, who visited Dr. Stone for several days, lays similar emphasis on the serious condition in which the doctor finds those who apply to her for treatment. "The cases which came to the dispensary were sorely in need of help. This was, I think, the invariable rule. Such cases they were as do not often come to the observance of physicians in this country, and some familiarity with the dispensaries of four of the large hospitals in New York City, has almost failed to show such need as the little doctor sees continually."

No physician in China can be a specialist. One of Dr. Stone's letters shows the variety of diseases which she is called upon to treat. "Women come to us almost dead; paralyzed, blind, and helpless . . . We have in the isolation wards, measles; and in the contagious rooms, locked up, leprosy; an insane woman locked up in her room; typhoid, tuberculosis, paralyzed women and children, ulcer cases such as you would never dream of, surgical cases of all kinds, and internal cases too numerous to mention."

A letter from a Kiukiang missionary tells of one woman who came to the hospital with "not a square inch of good flesh on her entire body." Fingers and toes were so diseased as to be dropping off, and the poor woman's suffering was unspeakable. Dr. Stone put her in isolation, and taking every precaution with gloves and antiseptics, herself washed and dressed the repulsive sores, in spite of the sufferer's protests, "Oh, doctor, don't touch me. I am too filthy for your pure hands to touch." This she did every day, until, her sores completely healed, the woman was discharged from the hospital a few weeks later.

Hon. Charles M. Dow of Jamestown, N.Y., who was taking a trip around the world, met Bishop Lewis on a Yangtse-kiang steamer, and was invited by him to stop off at Kiukiang to make the acquaintance of a remarkable surgeon of that city. Great was Mr. Dow's astonishment when the surgeon appeared and proved to be "a small and very attractive native Chinese woman."

Dr. Stone is so small that she has to stand on a stool to reach her operating table; but Dr. Danforth's testimony is that she is performing the largest operations known to surgery, and that no Chicago surgeon is doing work superior to hers. Moreover she has no fellow physicians to assist her in her surgical work. The most delicate operations, for which an American surgeon would call in the assistance of brother physicians, internes, and the most expert of graduate nurses, are performed by Dr. Stone entirely unaided except for the faithful nurses whom she has herself trained. Only at rare intervals does she receive a visit from a fellow physician such as Dr. Perkins of New York, who, in an interesting account of his stay at Kiukiang, tells of performing his first major operation "in her operating room and under her direction."

At first the people were afraid to submit to operations, but the doctor's marked success with those who permitted her to operate soon overcame their fear. The results of her skilful use of the knife have been most marvellous to them. That a young woman of over twenty, who could not be betrothed because of a hare lip reaching into the nose, with a projection of the maxillary bone between the clefts, could be successfully operated on and transformed into a marriageable maiden, seemed nothing short of miraculous. Nor was it less wonderful to them that an old woman could, by an operation, be relieved of an abdominal tumor from which she had suffered for sixteen years, and which, when removed, weighed fifty-two pounds. "The people appreciate surgery more and more," reads one of Dr. Stone's recent letters. "A lot of the tuberculosis patients who have seen the quick results from operations want me to operate on their lungs."

Another large department of Dr. Stone's work has been the training of her nurses. This has been an absolute necessity, for, as Dr. Stone said: "When I found I had to run a hospital with accommodations for 100 beds, and an out-patient department with sometimes 120 patients a day, I at once found I had to multiply myself by training workers. These workers I selected from various Christian schools with good recommendations as to qualifications. I do not dare to take into training any one who has failed as a teacher or in any line of work, because nursing is an art still in its embryo. To succeed in this profession one must not only know how to read and write, but also know arithmetic and some English."

The course of study which Dr. Stone gives her nurses is about the same as that prescribed by the regular training schools, or hospitals, in America. To do this she has had to translate several English text-books into Chinese for the use of her students. The reliable and efficient nurses who have completed the course and are now her trusted assistants in all her work, have amply repaid her for all the time and labour she has expended upon this part of her work.

In an article on "Hospital Economics" she speaks of the efficient service of these nurses:

"I am blessed with five consecrated young women," she says, "who have completed a course of nursing and studies with me, and I have divided the work into different departments, holding them responsible for the work and for the younger nurses under them. For instance, one of the graduates is the matron, who looks after all the housekeeping and the accounts, watching for the best market time for buying each article in connection with the diet, the best foodstuff for the money expended, and looks after each and all of the servants so that they do their work properly. Another graduate nurse looks after the dispensary, the filling of prescriptions, the weighing and compounding of medicines, and superintends the sale of drugs in that department. Another one has charge of all in-patients upstairs, and another downstairs, including private cases, with junior nurses under her. These look after the special diet, and the carrying out of orders in all the wards and the charting of records. (This is done in English.) Still another nurse has charge of the operating room, with all of the sterilization necessary for all major and minor operations, the distillation of water, and the responsibility of going out to cases with the doctor. In this way it is arranged that in case of all operations the one doctor has her assistants in the operating room, and yet does not interfere with the regular working of the hospital."

"Dr. Stone is multiplying herself many-fold by her splendid training of nurses in the Kiukiang hospital," is the verdict of Mrs. Bashford, wife of the Methodist Missionary Bishop of China. She has watched Dr. Stone's work with keen and intelligent interest, and her opinion seems to be justified by the results. When after weeks of unusual strain Dr. Stone was persuaded to take a short vacation in the mountains back of Kiukiang, her corps of fourteen nurses, five of them graduates, kept up the work of the hospital, and treated about eighty patients a day in the dispensary. Twice, in answer to telegrams, Dr. Stone returned to Kiukiang, only to find each time that everything had been done to her entire satisfaction. "Were it not for the efficient help I have from my nurses, I should not be able to manage this work at all," she says.

Doubtless one great reason for Dr. Stone's success in raising up efficient workers is her confidence in them, and her sympathetic attitude toward them. "I believe many a valued worker is lost to her profession through lack of sympathy and encouragement when needed," she once said. "Surely the Lord values the workers as well as His work, and we who want our work to prosper cannot afford to ignore the interests of those upon whom we depend so largely for success."

The nurses in turn have a pride in the hospital as great as the doctor's own, and are as devoted to it. "The nurses are fine in standing up for our standard of cleanliness," Dr. Stone wrote to a fellow-physician. "For instance, when this patient came (a very poor woman) the nurses got hold of her, bathed her, and put her in our clean, white clothes and tucked her away in one of these clean white beds in no time . . . She begged to keep the bandages on her bound feet. 'No,' the nurses said, 'such dirty bandages in our clean bed! No!'"

Writing to Dr. Danforth of her first graduating class, Dr. Stone said: "You may ask if they are going to run away and earn large sums for themselves. No, they are going to stay and help me in the hospital work, or earn money for the hospital. You see, I assign each one to a department of work, and she is the head-nurse of that department. Then by turn I send them out to do private nursing, and the sums they earn are turned into the hospital for caring for the poor who cannot help themselves. Mrs. Wong is nursing Mrs. B—of our own mission at Nanking, and when she comes back Miss Chang will be sent to Wuhu to nurse a lady of another mission. Dr. Barrie, of Kuling, has written to me to engage several for the new hospital at Kuling for foreigners during this summer season. I told him I could accommodate him because I have three other classes in training . . . The spirit has been most beautiful among the nurses. Many of them take their afternoon 'off duty' to do evangelistic work in the homes of patients."

The well-trained corps of nurses is one of the most convincing testimonies to that of which the whole hospital is a proof—the administrative ability of the physician in charge. No detail of a well-managed hospital, from the record files and wheel stretchers to the hand-power washing machine, is neglected. Nevertheless the hospital is conducted with true economy. Dr. Stone defines economy as "the art which avoids all waste and extravagance and applies money to the best advantage. It is not economy to buy cheap furniture that has to be replaced all the time. It is poor economy to buy cheap food and let patients suffer for lack of nourishment . . . It is poor economy to use cheap drugs and drug your patient's life out. It is poor economy to use wooden beds and have to patronize Standard Oil to keep them clean. It is also poor economy not to use sheets and thin quilts, instead of the heavy comfortables the Chinese have, just in order to save the heavy washing and disinfection. It is poor economy to have cheap servants who can do nothing. With trained workers to look after instruments, instead of having to depend on servants, I find instruments last longer." As a result, the universal testimony of those who visit the hospital is, "Dr. Stone has one of the finest hospitals we have ever seen."

From the outset the doctor's ideal has been to make the medical work as largely self-supporting as possible. Of course many of those most in need of medical aid could pay nothing for it, nor for their medicines, nor even, if they were in-patients, for their food. Others, however, could pay something, and still others were able to pay in full. Soon after work in the Danforth Hospital was begun, Dr. Stone wrote: "Our ordinary charge for food is sixty cash a day or two dollars per month. For private rooms they pay ten to twenty dollars, according to the kind of room they have. Occasionally we meet some generous Chinese who give freely and thus help a great deal our poor patients, some of whom cannot even pay for their rice. For instance, one man has paid three hundred dollars this year for his wife, who is still here for treatment, and will probably give more when she is through. Another man has given one hundred and forty dollars for his wife's treatment. Last quarter we received over four hundred dollars, and this quarter over five hundred dollars here. We are getting to have more of the well-to-do patients."

A letter written in 1905 tells of ways in which the Chinese assist the hospital financially: "It has been my privilege to minister unto many of this poor class of people with the fees I receive from the rich. So often I find in the morning I earn a good fee, and in the evening I spend it on a very poor case. Lately I have been sending a subscription book around. I first sent it to the highest official here, and it was immediately returned with fifty dollars. It encouraged me very much, for I know the work is approved of by the officials and the common people, and they are both helping all they can." Once she reported that at a time when the financial outlook was unusually discouraging, an unknown non-Christian Chinese sent a messenger several hundred *li* with a gift of money to relieve the situation.

Patients who cannot afford to pay anything, but who can use their hands, are given sewing to do, and in this way make some contribution toward the expenses of the work. The nurses, too, who have received training from the hospital, either give their services or the money which they receive from private cases. Thus, in various ways, many of the running expenses are met on the field, but as so much work is done for the poor, the physician's salary and the larger part of the equipment have come from friends in America.

Even in the interior of China, and in the midst of the most active of lives, Dr. Stone has never ceased to be a student. Early in her work she wrote to a friend in America who was also a physician, "We feel that in order to keep up in our profession we need occasionally some of the latest works, especially since medical science is one of the most progressive of all." Subsequent letters are full of commissions such as, "I need an English and Latin dictionary very much in the work. Will you buy one—a good one—for me?" "Will you kindly buy Hyde's work on 'Venereal Diseases,' not on Skin, for I have that." Or "I should like very much to have a work on Hygiene. You know the Chinese have such primitive ideas on that subject, and if I can get a good standard book I can pick out and translate for the benefit of the people. Then if there is still anything left, I would like a small book on bandaging and massage, for I want to train new nurses. Occasionally, when you see something new and well-tested, such as articles you think will help my work, especially anything on tuberculosis, cholera, hydrophobia, etc., etc., just remember the back number in China, won't you?"

With keen recognition of the inestimable value which her scientific study and training have been to her in her work, Dr. Stone has never failed to remember the great Source of motive and power, and has ever been eager to share with her patients the joy and peace of the Christian religion. Every morning she conducts a service in the hospital chapel for the employees of the hospital, and such of the patients as are able to attend. At the same time the nurses are holding a similar service in the ward upstairs. While the dispensary patients are waiting their turn in the examining room, one or more Bible women utilize the time by telling them the truths of Christianity. Dr. Stone's own mother has done such work for years, morning after morning, among her daughter's dispensary patients.

One of the other missionaries at Kiukiang tells of going through the hospital one evening, as the nurses were getting the patients settled for the night. She noticed a low murmur which she did not at first understand, until she saw that at every bed someone was in prayer. Here a mother was kneeling by the side of her little suffering son; there another mother of high rank was praying that the life of the baby by whose crib she knelt might be spared to her. In one corner a woman had crept out of bed and was kneeling with her face to the floor; in other places those who were too sick to leave their beds were softly praying in them.

The nurses are all Christian women, able to minister to the spiritual as well as the physical. Dr. Perkins says of them: "The nurses, too, are strongly evangelistic in their thought and effort, and even to one who could not understand the language, the atmosphere of Christian harmony and the remarkable lack of friction in a place so busy and so constantly full of problems, was very noticeable."

One night Dr. Stone went into the room of a patient who had been greatly dreading a serious operation which she was to undergo the next day, to be greeted with a radiant face and the words, "Oh, doctor, I'm not afraid now of the operation. I've been talking to your God." Earlier in the evening one of the youngest of the nurses had found her crying bitterly and the old woman had told her: "I'm so afraid of the operation. You see the other woman you told me of was a Christian and of course your God helped her. I've never worshipped your God. I never knew of Him before and He may not help me." "Why, you needn't cry over that!" the little nurse assured her. "Our God doesn't blame you when no one had told you about Him. Now that you know, if you love Him and pray to Him, He will help you." Then she knelt down beside her and taught her how to pray to Him. After the operation was over and the patient, fully recovered, was going back to her village, she said to the doctor, "I am the first one in our village to hear of Jesus. Won't you come *soon* to my people and tell them."

Dr. Stone's letters and reports are full of accounts of the way in which, from the beginning, the work of the hospital has brought the knowledge of the Great Physician to those whose bodies had been so tenderly cared for by His followers that their hearts were very open. Whole families, sometimes almost entire communities, have become Christian as a result of the medical work. An interesting instance of the way in which the hospital's influence is spread by its patients is the case of a little girl, eight years old, who unbound her feet while in the hospital, and became so ardent an advocate of natural feet that after she had returned to the village in which she lived, she and her father succeeded in persuading three hundred families to pledge that their daughters should have natural feet.

It is quite impossible to separate Dr. Stone's definitely religious work from her medical work; for while Sunday afternoons and the chapel hour in the morning are set aside by her for purely evangelistic work, her Christian faith permeates all that she does. In the first years of her practice she did some itinerating work, but now that the work is so large and she is the only physician in charge, she has had to give that up. The nurses, however, still carry it on. "You see, while I am practically tied to the place," writes the doctor, "it gives so much happiness to be able to send out workers like these and to spread our influence. As the nurses say, they will be able to send a lot of patients back to the hospital. You see the more work we have the merrier we are."

Every time an evangelistic worker goes out on the district, one of the nurses accompanies her, and with ointments, simple medicines, bandages, vaccine, etc., treats several hundred patients in the country beyond the reach of physicians. At one time in the bitter cold weather of winter a message came from a distant village where smallpox was raging, asking that a nurse be sent to treat the sick people and vaccinate those who had not yet taken the disease. One woman in that village had once been at the hospital, and it was through her that the call came. One of the nurses at once volunteered to go, and with a Bible woman and a reliable man-servant she took the trip down the river, in a little sampan, to the smitten village. During four days she treated over one hundred patients not only in the village, but also in the region round about; for she and the Bible woman walked thirty *li* every day to sufferers in the country. While the nurse worked, the Bible woman preached, and in this way hundreds of people heard of Christianity for the first time. As Dr. Stone says, "The cry now is not for open doors, for we have free entrance into the homes of the rich and poor. What we need now is an efficient force of trained evangelistic workers to . . . follow up the seed thus sown broadcast on such receptive soil." This need the Training School for Bible Women is helping to meet.

Mrs. Stephen Baldwin writing to Dr. Danforth said, "The Lord honoured your investment by placing in it one of the most wonderful doctors in all this world." But Dr. Stone is not only a physician, but an all-round woman. "She is equal to any sudden call to speak," said one who heard her often when she was in America. A report of the Missionary Conference at Kuling, China, states that "Dr. Stone's paper on 'Hospital Economics' was the finest feature of an attractive conference." At the request of this conference she prepared a leaflet on the diet suited to Chinese schoolgirls, and a few years ago wrote a very useful book on the subject: "Until the Doctor Comes."

"I observed her in her home," writes a missionary who stopped at Kiukiang for a few days *en route* to Peking, "a housewifely woman, thoughtful of every detail that might ensure a guest's comfort. In a single month recently she treated 1,995 women and children, yet she is not too busy to be a gracious hostess. Chinese ladies delight to visit her, and such is the influence of this modest woman that the Hsien's wife has unbound her feet."

It may well be questioned, great as are Dr. Stone's achievements, which is of more value, the actual work she is doing, or the inspiration which her efficient, self-sacrificing Christian life is bringing to the awakened womanhood of the new China. The words of Miss Howe regarding Dr. Stone and Dr. Kahn indicate their influence: "They seem to be an inspiration to the girls and women of all classes. When our schoolgirls learn of anything 'the doctors' did when they were pupils, they seem to think they have found solid ground on which to set their feet." A letter from another fellow-worker stated that Dr. Stone was to give the address at the graduation exercises of the class of 1909 of the Nanking Normal School for Women at which the viceroy and "other notables of China" were to be present. Dr. Stone was greatly touched when the daughter-in-law of a viceroy once said to her that she would gladly give up all her servants, her beautiful clothes, her jewels, even her position, if she could lead a useful life like hers, instead of making one of the many puppets in the long court ceremonies, with nothing to think of except her appearance, and nothing to do but kill time.

It is a great joy to the doctor to have a part in bringing about a realization of the achievements of which Chinese women are capable, and she has been willing to make any sacrifice necessary to do this. Soon after Dr. Kahn's transfer to Nanchang had left her with almost double work, Dr. Danforth wrote that he had found a nurse in one of the Chicago hospitals who was willing to go to China, and asked Dr. Stone what she would think of having her come to the Danforth Hospital. Dr. Stone replied that while she would take her if Dr. Danforth wished, she would really rather not, on the whole. Personally, she said, she would have been very glad to have her come, but she was eager that her work should accomplish two things which it could accomplish only if it were purely Chinese: first, that it should convince the Chinese women themselves that they are able to do things of which they have never dreamed; and, second, that it should show the people of other nations that the only reason why Chinese women have for centuries lived such narrow lives is that they have not had opportunity to develop their native powers. She feared that if an American nurse came to the hospital it would look as if the purely Chinese work had failed, and that it had been necessary to call in help from America.

Accordingly, although Dr. Stone has sometimes been forced to admit that her work has been so heavy as to tax both heart and strength to the utmost, she has carried it all these years with no help, except from the nurses she has trained. She has counted no task too hard, no labour too constant, if she may thereby benefit her countrywomen physically, intellectually, or spiritually. "She does not spare herself," one of her friends writes, "she seems unable to do so, and is too tender-hearted to turn the suffering away for her own need."

The past year has brought peculiar burdens to the doctor. She carried on her regular hospital work as usual, until the disturbances caused by the Revolution came so near that all the women and children in the schools and hospital were ordered into the foreign concession. This order came at night, and by two o'clock the next morning not a patient was left in the hospital.

Dr. Stone turned over the hospital to the revolutionary leaders, and each day she and her trained nurses cared for the injured soldiers sheltered in it. The leaders of the Revolution urged her to wear the white badge which was their emblem, but she told them that while her sympathies were with them, as a Red Cross physician she must remain neutral, that she might be able to render assistance to the wounded on both sides. Her explanation was courteously accepted, and an armed guard was furnished to escort her to and from the hospital each morning and evening.

When the Manchu governor of Nanchang was captured he was taken to Kiukiang, where, in chagrin at his imprisonment, he attempted suicide. Deserted by his servants and soldiers, he would have died alone and uncared for had it not been for Dr. Stone, for no one else dared to go near him. Dr. Stone and two of her nurses cared for him until the death which they could not prevent, but which they made far easier than it would otherwise have been. It was this same governor who, but a few months before, had refused Dr. Stone the rights of Chinese citizenship because, in purchasing land for a men's hospital at Kiukiang, she was buying property for foreigners.

When the leaders of the revolutionary party learned that their prisoner had committed suicide they were greatly disturbed. None of them dared to carry the news to General Ma, lest, in accordance with an old Oriental custom, he should punish the bearer of ill tidings. In their perplexity they went to Dr. Stone and asked her to take the news to the general. Accordingly the little doctor, accompanied only by one of her nurses, went to the general's headquarters to break the news to him. It is significant, not only of the universal respect accorded the doctor, but also of the new position accorded woman in China, that these women, who ventured unattended into a soldiers' camp, were received with every courtesy. General Ma asked the doctor many questions about her work, and at the close of their interview exclaimed, "When things are settled once more, I intend to find support for such a work; the Chinese ought to help it."

Because of the disturbances caused by the Revolution, many students in the Kiukiang schools returned to their homes. The family of one young woman insisted that she make use of this enforced vacation to become married to the young Chinese to whom she had long been engaged. The marriage was unwelcome to her, for she was a Christian and the man was not, but as she was the only Christian in her family she received no sympathy from them, and the wedding was set for Christmas day. The parents, however, yielded to their daughter's earnest desire for a Christian ceremony, and her brother was dispatched to Kiukiang to seek Dr. Stone, who had been eminently successful in all kinds of operations and might surely be relied upon to tie a satisfactory marriage knot. Dr. Stone accordingly left all her Christmas engagements, and accompanied by a Chinese pastor and one of her nurses, set out, through a heavy snow storm, for the girl's home. When the wedding guests were all assembled, Dr. Stone said that she would like to say a few words before the ceremony took place, and for an hour and a half she told her hearers of the Christian good tidings. The result was that when the wedding was over the mother and father of the bride brought their idols to her, and allowed their daughter to apply the match to them, for both had determined to become Christians. The father said that he wished other people to hear the good things Dr. Stone had told them, and would give the land for a Christian school. The bridegroom volunteered to do the carpenter work which would be necessary before a school could be opened, and now the young wife is teaching a group of children who have entered this new Christian school, and in the new home husband and wife daily unite in morning prayers.

After the Revolution was practically over, but conditions were still so unsettled as to make it unwise to reopen the hospital, Dr. Stone and several of her nurses made a trip to a number of towns in the region around Kiukiang. In a recent letter Dr. Stone tells of being given a piece of land by the influential people in one of these towns, with the earnest entreaty that she leave a nurse there to carry on a permanent medical work. She could make them no definite promise, but is hoping that friends in America will make it financially possible to support a nurse and dispensary where they are so greatly needed.

Truly the Chinese women are blessed in having so perfect an embodiment of the ideal woman of the great new China in this unassuming physician, whom a friend who has known her from babyhood declares to have the most perfect Christian character of any one she knows. After his visit in Kiukiang, Dr. Perkins exclaimed: "Such a wonderful woman as Dr. Mary Stone is! I do not know of any good quality she does not possess"; and one who has had an intimate acquaintance with the college women of America says: "What a marvel Dr. Stone is! To me she is unexcelled in charm, in singleness of purpose, and all-round efficiency, by any other woman I have ever known."

YU KULIANG

Yu Kuliang

The same year that little Mary Stone first saw the light, on almost the same day, in another part of the same city, another little girl was born, a member of the same proud old family whose line runs back so many years into Chinese antiquity. Unlike Mary Stone, she was not born into a Christian home, but it was a home where the parents truly loved each other, and one in which she might have spent a very happy childhood, had not the young father died while she was still a baby.

The mother, broken-hearted over her husband's death, decided to become a Taoist nun and devote the remainder of her life to the search for truth. With her baby she shut herself up in a little hut outside of the city, seeing no one, and giving her whole time to the care of the child and her efforts to find truth. The members of her family, which is one of the wealthiest and most aristocratic in Kiukiang, were greatly pleased with what they considered an eminently virtuous resolve for a young widow to make, and applied to the Emperor for his approval of the course she had decided to follow. This being heartily given, they built a very comfortable home for her on the outskirts of Kiukiang. The building was christened Purity Hall, and over its gateway were placed large placards announcing the imperial sanction of the life which the young widow had chosen for herself and her child.

Here the little girl grew to womanhood, knowing no companionship except that of her mother and her teachers. Her mother employed the best possible Chinese teachers for her, and she early learned to read the books of the three religions of China, that she might join her mother in her pursuit of truth. She seldom left the house, and no one but her teachers ever entered it, but day after day she pored over the books on Taoism, Buddhism, and Confucianism until she had read them all. She, too, became a Taoist nun, but continued in the worship and study of Buddhism and Confucianism also, determined to find the *true* religion.

She even surpassed her mother in the ardour of her search for truth, for she spent twelve entire years, in periods of three years each, in one room of the house, living in the most absolute seclusion, not seeing her mother, speaking to no one, and hearing no voice, for three years at a time. After such a vigil she came out into the rest of the house for a year, then went back for another three years of solitude. In one corner of this room were the shrine and the altar before which Yu Kuliang knelt hour after hour during the years of her long vigil, and the idols, large and small, of wood and stone, which were her only companions. She always kept three sticks of incense burning before the shrine, one for each religion, that she might be sure not to make a mistake. In the ardour of her devotion she even made offerings of pieces of her own flesh to the idols. Her whole body, even her face, was covered with the ugly round scars caused by this self-mutilation.

When Yu Kuliang was a woman of thirty-two she learned that the Stones were her cousins, and of her own accord went to call on them. Thereafter the doors of "Purity Hall," so long fast closed to all, were thrown open to the Stone family. Yu Kuliang and her cousin Dr. Mary Stone, born at almost the same time, living, and having always lived, lives as totally different as two lives could be, became fast friends. To Dr. Stone, Yu Kuliang frankly confessed that an entire life spent in seeking truth had not brought her success. She was very willing to listen to all that Dr. Stone had to tell her of the truth which she had found, and finally even succeeded in summoning up sufficient courage to attend the Sunday morning church service. Her years of seclusion had made her so timid, and so afraid of mingling among people, however, that the first time she came to the church she disguised herself in the garb of a Chinese man. Dr. Stone gave her a Bible and she began the study of it at once, with the same earnestness and determination to find truth that she had shown in her study of the books of the Chinese religion.

After she had once gained courage to attend the church service she came frequently, no longer in man's clothes, nor in the coarse, grey cotton costume of the Taoist nun, which she discarded soon after knowing Dr. Stone, but in the ordinary dress of the Chinese woman. She became a frequent visitor to the hospital, too, where she loved to follow Dr. Stone from ward to ward, or to sit beside her in the dispensary as she cared for the suffering women and children who flocked there daily.

Finally Dr. Stone invited her to come to her for a week's visit, hardly daring to hope that she would do so; for she had never, since entering "Purity Hall" as a baby, spent a night outside of it. But she consented, and gladly drank in all that Dr. Stone and the doctor's mother told her of the truth which she had so long sought. One day soon after she had gone home, when Dr. Stone was calling on her and her mother, the mother drew Dr. Stone aside and said, "Since my daughter came back from your house she hasn't been upstairs to see the idols once." After years of ceaseless devotion to them, Yu Kuliang had forsaken her idols, and was turning toward the living God. Soon afterward, when it was necessary for Dr. Stone to go to America for an operation, and for Miss Hughes, who was in charge of the Bible Woman's Training School, to accompany her, Yu Kuliang came and asked that she might enter the school when Miss Hughes returned from America. But when Dr. Stone and Miss Hughes returned to China, they found Yu Kuliang suffering from tuberculosis. The long years of self-inflicted imprisonment had left her with no vitality to resist, and the disease was making rapid progress.

Soon after the doctor's return, Yu Kuliang's mother went away for a visit of some days. One afternoon during her absence, when Dr. Stone and Miss Hughes were calling on Yu Kuliang, she told them that she was studying the Bible, and trying to pray, and added: "I never go near the idols any more. They are all upstairs in my old cell." Dr. Stone at once said: "If you no longer believe in the idols, get rid of them. Give them to us." Yu Kuliang assented immediately, saying, "Take them if you want to," and went upstairs with Dr. Stone to get them. They brought down a Buddha and a goddess of mercy, which, after a few moments of further talk and prayer, Dr. Stone and Miss Hughes took away with them, Yu Kuliang watching them without a murmur.

The next day Dr. Stone and her mother went to see Yu Kuliang again, and with her consent and approval chopped to pieces a huge wooden idol, which was too large to carry away. When they were wondering what they should do with the stump of the body, Yu Kuliang exclaimed, "Throw the horrid thing into the ditch!" Thus passed out of her life the idols to which she had prayed for hours at a time, before which she had burned numberless sticks of incense, beside which she had lived and slept, and which she had made her most constant companions all the years of her life. The old temple bell, which had for years been used to call the gods from sleep, was given to Dr. Stone on the same day.

But when Yu Kuliang's mother returned she was furiously angry—not at the daughter to whom she was devoted, but at those who had turned her away from her idols. Dr. Stone took the old woman's hands in hers and pleaded with her: "You know your daughter does not believe in idols, you know the misery of her life, you know how she longs for peace; and as long as you harbour the idols in your home, Jesus cannot come into her heart and dwell there." The old woman at once broke out, in the tones of one taking the part of an injured friend, "But if your God is such a mighty one, and has the tens of thousands of followers you tell us He has, why should He be jealous of our poor little idols and those who worship them?"

Dr. Stone did not interrupt the tirade which was now poured forth, but picked up a piece of wood and a pebble from the floor, and when the old woman waited for her to answer, quietly replied to the pebble and bit of wood in her hand. Finally the woman said, "Why don't you answer me? You have come to see me, and perhaps I have been rude, but you are my relative and I want to be friends with you." Still Dr. Stone did not answer, but went on talking to the stone and wood, until the old woman lost patience and exclaimed, "What nonsense is this!"

Then Dr. Stone put her arm around her and answered, "If you think it is nonsense for me to talk to the stone and wood in your house, instead of giving you attention, how do you think the Heavenly Father feels,—the one who created you, the one who is your Father—when you satisfy yourself with images of wood and stone instead of giving that love and devotion to Him?" Before Dr. Stone left the young women knelt in prayer, but the mother would not join them.

Later, with her mother's consent, Yu Kuliang went to the hospital, and there spent four of the ten last days of her life, in the companionship of her cousin. Dr. Stone gave her every minute that could be spared from her hospital duties, telling her of the glad new life which she was soon to enter, and praying with her. Many times Yu Kuliang tried to leave the bed to kneel with Dr. Stone, but the doctor explained to her that her prayers were just as acceptable where she was, and that she was too weak to kneel. "Those four days in the hospital with cousin were the happiest in my life," she told her mother when she returned to her home.

When she knew that she could not get well she insisted, weak as she was, upon being dressed and having her photograph taken, for all the photographs which she had had before were in the dress of the Taoist nun, and she wanted to have one taken after she had become a Christian.

Just before her death she said to her mother, "Mother, there is nothing in this life of ours, nothing! We were all wrong. I'm so glad it is over and now I am not at all afraid, for I am going to that beautiful place." And then, her lifelong quest at length crowned with success, she went to behold the face of Him who is the Truth.

ANNA STONE

Anna Stone

I

EAGER FOR EDUCATION

"God knew where to send girls; He knew who would be good to them," Mrs. Stone assured the neighbours who had come to condole with her on the birth of a second daughter, and to remind her that "ten queenly daughters are not worth as much as one son with a limp." Years before, when the baby's father, one of the literati, had lost all his property in the Tai Ping Rebellion, he had adopted the profession of teaching Chinese to the missionaries, as the only dignified means by which one of his rank and learning could earn a living. While he taught them Chinese characters, they taught him about Christianity, and it was not long before he was in charge of a Christian chapel in Kiukiang. So when this little daughter was born, she was given the good old Bible name of Anna, and great plans were laid for her future. While she was still a tiny baby her mother carried her to the missionary in charge of the girls' boarding school, one of those to whom her father had taught the Chinese language years before, and said to her, "As soon as this baby is old enough, I want you to take her and train her for Christian work."

If she was to fulfil her mother's ambition for her Anna must of course receive an education, although a girl who could read or write even the simplest sentence was then almost unknown in China. But Mrs. Stone knew well that the more education Anna had, the more efficient a worker she would be. She herself had never been taught at all, and after she had become a Christian and was eager to tell other women of the good news which she had learned, she had found herself sadly hampered because she could not read the Bible. It was not so difficult when her husband was at home to read it for her; but while he was away on his preaching tours, she had lost many opportunities of teaching Christianity to the women who came to see her, because of her inability to read the Book which told of the great new truth she had learned. So, busy as she was with her babies and her household cares, she determined to learn to read, and asked her husband to teach her.

Pastor Stone, however, had still something to learn. He did not believe that it was possible for the feminine mind, especially that of a woman grown, to learn the difficult Chinese characters; and he told his wife that, in his opinion, it was not worth while for her to attempt it. If Mother Stone was discouraged she did not show it. Every night after the rest of the family were asleep she set a candle beside her bed and studied characters diligently. Whenever Pastor Stone woke up for a moment, or turned over in bed, he would receive a gentle nudge and Mother Stone would delightedly exclaim, "Oh, father, won't you please tell me what this character is?" He soon decided to teach her in orthodox fashion, and she proved to be such an apt pupil that it was not long before she was in charge of a little day school for girls.

Anna received much of her early education from her mother, and for a time she and her older sister Mary went to school with their brother. Girls at school were decidedly a novelty, and the visiting mandarin opened his eyes in amazement. "Can *girls* learn anything?" he demanded of the teacher, who was forced to admit that they learned as fast as the boys, and sometimes a little faster. When a little older, Anna became a member of the Kiukiang Boarding School for girls, where she proved to be a diligent and quick pupil. During this time her sister Mary went to America to take her medical course, and down in her heart Anna cherished a secret hope that when she had completed her high school work she, too, might go to that wonderful Christian country from which her missionary teachers had come and in which her sister was receiving the training which would fit her for such large service among her countrywomen. She said very little about this hope to any one, but she and her friend I-lien Tang, who was also eager to go to America, determined to pray about it, and to study so faithfully that if the way should ever open for them to go, they would be ready. Accordingly they completed the high school course in Chinese, and studied English and Latin in addition.

In 1898 Bishop Joyce, of the Methodist Church, and his wife took a trip to the Orient to visit the mission stations. While in Kiukiang they became so much interested in the two girls, Anna Stone and I-lien Tang, that they offered to take them back to America with them. The autumn of 1898 therefore found Anna in America, the country of her dreams, and a student in Hamline University. She entered into her college work with much enthusiasm and made excellent progress in it. She was not strong, however, and was so far from well at the end of the year that it seemed best for her to relinquish her plan of following in her sister's footsteps by taking a medical course. She therefore planned to fit herself for some other form of service which would involve less physical strain, and left Hamline, after having been there only one year. But she left behind her many warm friends among the students, some of whom had become Christians as a result of the consistent and beautiful Christian life of this young Chinese girl.

The next autumn Anna entered Folts Mission Institute, where arrangements were made for her to take the two years' Bible course in three years, in the hope that she might thus regain her health. Her teachers testify that she was a brilliant student, and that her English was so perfect that one who heard her, without seeing her, would never have known that she was a foreigner. When one of them once asked her how it was that she had such a correct pronunciation, she said that when she was in Kiukiang Boarding School she used to watch the lips of the missionaries when they were speaking English, in order to see just how the words were formed.

Her use of words, too, was almost as accurate as her enunciation of them, although occasionally the intricacies of the English language proved somewhat mystifying. For example, when she was at her doctor's office one day he asked if he had given her any medicine when she was there before.

"No, doctor, you gave me a proscription," she answered. The doctor's smile showed her that she had made a mistake, and as soon as they were outside she asked the teacher who was with her what she ought to have said.

"*Pre*scription, *pre*scription," she repeated. "I must remember that. What was it we had in church last Sunday? Was that a prescription or a proscription?"

"That was a subscription," the teacher told her.

"Oh, yes, a subscription. But what did you call the writing on the stones in the graveyard? Was that a prescription or a subscription?"

"That was an inscription," was the answer, and perhaps it is small wonder that Anna exclaimed in despair, "Oh, this terrible English! Can I ever get it!"

On the whole, however, she was very much at home with the English language. One morning as she was going down to breakfast some one asked, "How is our little China girl this morning?" "Neither cracked nor broken!" was her instant response.

During all her stay in America she was in great demand as a speaker, and did as much of this work as her health permitted, always giving her message in English, and everywhere winning friends for herself and her loved people. "Those who have watched her as she held the attention of large audiences with the simple story of her own people, will not soon forget the modest, unassuming girl who touched their lives for a brief hour," says one who heard her often.

When she entered Folts Institute it was thought that it would be a good thing for her to take vocal lessons to strengthen her throat and lungs. This training was given simply for the sake of her health, and with no expectation that she would ever sing in public, but it soon became evident that she had musical ability of no small degree. Her voice was very sweet, and had such a power to capture the hearts of her hearers that she was given the title of the "Sweet Singer," and was in great demand for meetings large and small. The whole energy of her life was so given to her Master that this newly discovered gift was at once consecrated wholly to His service. "You may think me narrow," she said earnestly, when her teacher proposed that she should study some nature songs, "but I feel that I must be the girl of one song." And into the one song, the Christian hymn, she put her whole soul, as any who heard her sing, "I love to tell the story," "Faith of our fathers," or the one that she perhaps sang most often, "Saved by Grace," will testify.

"I can hear her still as she sang 'Saved by Grace' to the large audience of the General Executive in 1902," wrote one, several years later. "She put such fulness of meaning and power into this simple song. It was a part of her own experience." Another said,

"I heard her sing 'I love to tell the story' to an audience of over five hundred college girls at the student conference of the Young Women's Christian Association at Silver Bay, and the effect was wonderful."

It had been the thought of the principal of Folts Institute that the cost of Anna's musical education should be defrayed by gifts from friends who were interested in her and her work. But after one spring vacation, when Anna had been addressing several meetings and had been given quite a little money, she went to the principal's office and turned over the entire amount which she had received. "But this is twice as much as your lessons for the year will cost, Anna," the principal told her, and started to hand back half of it. But Anna would not take it, and insisted that it be used to pay for the piano lessons of another Chinese student at the Institute. "I don't want—to get into debt," she said.

While studying at Folts Institute Anna's first great sorrow came to her in the death of her father. They had always been comrades, and she had often accompanied him on his preaching tours into the country. It was on one of these tours, made during the time of the Boxer uprising, that Pastor Stone received the injuries at the hands of a mob which were probably the cause of his death. The news was a great blow to Anna, but she bore it quietly and bravely, and when a few days later it was her turn to lead the students' prayer meeting, she chose "Heaven" for her topic. "Before I came to your country, I used to think it was heaven," she said; "but now I am so glad it isn't, for then they might try to keep father out, and now I know he is inside."

She completed her course at Folts Institute in 1902, and as she seemed in good health, entered Central Wesleyan College for further training. But her zeal for her work always led her to overestimate her own strength, and her patience in suffering and desire not to cause any one any trouble, made it hard for others to know the true state of her health. One of her teachers at Folts says that Anna would often be ill for days before any one would have any knowledge of it, so uncomplaining was she. This teacher tells how at one time, when Anna finally had to give up, the tears rolled down the cheeks of the girl who bore pain so bravely that it was unsuspected even by those who were watching her carefully, at the thought that the friend to whom she gave both the century-old reverence of the Chinese for a teacher and the warm love of her grateful heart, should have to minister to her needs. It was found, after she had been at the Central Wesleyan College for a few months, that courageous as she was, her strength was not sufficient to enable her to go on with her studies.

She spent the rest of the year in Minneapolis in the home of her good friends, Bishop and Mrs. Joyce. She was never content to be idle, and after a few months of rest she gave several addresses in the churches of Minnesota and North Dakota, awakening interest in the cause she represented wherever she went. She so won the hearts of the young people that when she went back to China it was as the representative of the young women who formed the Standard Bearer Society of the Minneapolis branch of the Woman's Foreign Missionary Society.

In the summer of 1903 a specialist pronounced her to be suffering from tuberculosis, and the next winter was spent in southern California in the hope that in that favourable climate she might be cured. Even here her eagerness to serve her people led her to do as much speaking as her physician would permit. But she was anxious to get to the work for which these years of preparation had been spent, and with hopeful and eager expectation she sailed for China on the S.S. *Siberia*, June 11, 1904.

II

AMONG HER OWN PEOPLE

On her return to her own country, Anna began her work with great enthusiasm. The spirit with which she entered into it is shown in her report of the first year's work: "After six years of special preparation, for which I feel greatly indebted to my Master, it is a happy privilege to do what may be in my power to show Him my gratitude. The blessings I received from the hands of those who gave cheerfully for His sake, I will endeavour to pass on to others. During those years of absorption in study there were times when I was anxious for others to share with me the joy which comes from the Christian faith, but the real opportunity did not appear until last July when I returned to my home land. With gladness and thanksgiving I entered into the work already well and carefully organized by my senior missionaries."

The evangelistic work for women, of which she was put in charge, offered a large and varied field for service. "The success which my sister has had in her profession gives me easy access to many classes of our people," she reported soon after her return. Among the hospital and dispensary patients she found one of her greatest opportunities. She was not only able to reach those who came for treatment, but through them she had access to their homes, and spent a large part of her time in visiting among them and in entertaining guests in her own home. "Many know of the hospital and of the lady physician, and come to see the work, and daily we cordially welcome such guests into our home," a letter reads. "There are times when I walk with my sister on the street, and the ladies call the doctor in. Thus I gain access to friendly homes."

She was untiring in her efforts to fit herself to make use of every opportunity which presented itself, never regarding her preparation for service as completed, but always eager to learn any new thing which would help her. A letter written soon after beginning her work tells of one of the means by which she sought to increase her usefulness: "I think it is imperative for me to study something more of the Chinese classics. The little knowledge I have, God has helped me to use for His glory, and a knowledge of the classical sayings will enable me at least to approach the educated classes on a common ground, and to induce them to see that which they know not, from that which they do know."

During her first year of work she had four Bible women associated with her who went out with her daily, conducting meetings for women in the two chapels which were under her direction, visiting in the homes, or talking to patients in the dispensary waiting room. One of her early letters reads: "I felt that these Bible women needed special hours for prayer and Bible study, in order to give out the Bread of Life to others. So arrangements were made to have at least two hours of study every Monday morning, and we have prayer together before planning to carry out the Lord's will in the week's work."

In addition to this work she was given oversight of the two day schools for girls in Kiukiang. Of them she reported: "The teachers are trying to do their best, but many times I have wished that we could secure better educated women and have our day school standard advanced. The girls who can afford to go to school don't care to study the old Chinese books which these women are prepared to teach, so the better classes are not being touched by the Christian teachers. Those who have nothing special for the girls to do let them go to while away the time; then when tea picking time comes they leave the school. All can see that such work cannot be of any great value."

Conditions of this sort were discouraging indeed, but she met the situation with characteristic courage, and added to her other duties the task of teaching a little music and English in these schools. The introduction of these subjects proved to be very successful in reviving the pupils' flagging interest. "The girls are more interested just now," a letter says, "because they have once a week a lesson in singing; formerly it was given on Saturday in our home, but experience soon taught me that this was an impossibility on account of the continuous callers and disturbances. I go now to each school once a week and teach them there. They also have a lesson in English during the week. It seems so strange to me that all people, old and young, male and female, are seeking a knowledge of English."

She was quick to see, however, that the only permanently successful solution of the day school problem was in well-trained teachers. Her great desire was for "the day when day school teachers should be better qualified for their work, that they might draw pupils to school by their own knowledge." In the meantime she did all she could to add to the efficiency of the teachers she had. One of her letters tells of her efforts to help one of her discouraged assistants: "One of the teachers is very anxious and feels that she cannot teach the school. She spoke to me several times of her inability to keep the pupils' attention because of her own lack of knowledge. As we have no trained teachers to take her place I cannot spare her. Though she has not a good head she has a good Christian heart, so for the good of the school I have to keep her and give her a few lessons each week. It is doing her good and helping her to teach better."

Again she reported the following year, "A special effort was made to throw away the old, parrot-like way of learning. As the teachers needed instruction as well as the pupils, sometimes, the text-books were taken away. The teachers were required to tell a story every day; and with the story a verse of the Scriptures, meant for a peg on which to hang the tale, was committed to memory by the girls. The teacher would write six easy characters each afternoon on the blackboard for the girls to copy before going home. Thus the girls learned how to listen, to memorize, and to write. Since the number of girls increases perceptibly when we have a little English I use it as a bait. By Miss Merrill's consent, help was secured from the boarding-school in teaching half an hour of English every day in the two city schools."

In December of 1904, at the annual meeting of the Central China Methodist Mission, Miss Stone was given the entire charge of the Bible Women's Training School. A letter to a friend shows the keen delight with which she entered upon this new work: "I am enjoying the work very much," she wrote. "It seems so strange to me that these women are like my old friends. They are free and at home with me, and I can say already that I love them . . . I wish you could be here just to look at them and see how willing they are to be taught." It was her desire to live in the school that she might share the life of the women outside of class hours, but after a few days' trial this proved too wearing, and the doctor insisted upon her giving it up, greatly to her own disappointment and that of the women.

She was very eager that these women, all of whom were from families of small means, and were supported by scholarships while at the school, should do something towards meeting at least a part of their expenses. A few months after she had taken charge of the work she joyfully wrote Mrs. Joyce:

> "An industrial department is actually started, and we have found it helpful to a great many. We are not attempting fancy things, but we strive to make useful articles and things that we use ourselves, or for sale. So far we have made only babies' shoes, which we sold to foreigners living at Kuling, and some hemstitched handkerchiefs, and some plain knitting. Each one of them is given fifty cash a month for spending money, and it will leave a good balance for the school. They work from three to five P.M., so their studies are not neglected thereby. This work means also a livelihood to a poor old lady . . . She was in the hospital for over three years, living on the charity money the doctor earned. I felt that she could be more useful and happy by teaching sewing, since she is a beautiful needle worker, so the school boards her and gets her teaching for the women. I have been quite happy in this work, because I feel the women are learning self-respect and to look upon manual labour as something honourable. I have a chance to tell them about the American ideas, how American people despise begging but would work with pride in any position, for an honest living."

In the growth of the women she found her greatest joy. "The women are learning," she said in the same letter, "and I feel that God is making them zealous for the souls of others. I watch anxiously for improvements in their characters and two or three of them give me secret pleasure by their signs of unselfishness and spiritual growth."

Another letter to Mrs. Joyce tells of the way in which the members of the Training School were given practical work in connection with their studies: "Every day I call upon the farther advanced pupils to work. Two go out with the girls to teach in the two day schools of the city, the other two take charge of the industrial work. So every afternoon they have two hours of work to do. On Sunday I send them to the two chapels in the morning and I go with the first two one week and with the other two the next week. On every Tuesday I send out all women except three, at three o'clock, to invite our neighbours to our class-meeting. The three who stay at home are to entertain those who come. Every Tuesday we get from twenty to forty outsiders to listen to the gospel. Yesterday afternoon several pupils told the guests how they learned to know the loving Father." One of her former teachers at Folts Institute, who visited her at this time, wrote that she knew not which to admire more, "the whole-souled devotion of the teacher, or that of the women students."

Miss Stone's health did not permit her to do as much itinerant work as she desired, but in the summer of 1905, during the vacation of the Bible Women's Training School, she made a trip of some weeks, visiting every station in the district. Itinerating in China is a process worthy of its name, as all bedding, food, and housekeeping materials must be carried along. But Anna was feeling well, and the very day after the work of the Training School closed she and her mother set out. At every city she reported that they "had a very good opportunity to work among the women," or that "many women showed a great interest in listening." Her father had been the first Christian preacher at one place which they visited, and had worked there for many years; another city was that in which the Stone's old family homestead was located, so she and her mother were sure of a welcome. "We had hardly any time to ourselves," she wrote. "So many people came to see us, and mistook me for my sister. Mother welcomed all callers and talked with them most of the time. Among these there were people from the opposite village who came over to destroy our house in 1900. I think they are quite ashamed of the act now."

Busy as she was, meeting and talking to the people who everywhere came to greet her and her mother, Anna's mind was not so wholly occupied with the present that she was oblivious to the future. On her return she made several valuable suggestions for the development of the work in the various places, such as that the chapel in one city be moved to a more central location, that a vacant piece of property belonging to the mission would be an excellent site for a day school for girls, etc. "There ought to be a school in Whang Mai as a centre for women to work in," her report reads. "There are many women in that city who are friendly to the church . . . When my parents were there there were quite a few women as members of the church, but now they don't come to church, because there is no woman to talk to them." She summed up the impressions of her trip in the words, "The trip opened my eyes to the fact that the harvest is 'truly plenteous' and the labourers are sadly few." At the same time her faith added, "But I am so glad to know that my Master is before us who are few in number."

III

THE POWER OF AN ENDLESS LIFE

It is not surprising that with all her interests Anna Stone longed to live and make use of the unusual opportunities which she had received. "If God is willing I hope to work many years yet for Him," she wrote Mrs. Joyce after she had been back in China a few months; and at the end of her second year's work she said: "There are many things for which I am very thankful in the past year, but perhaps the greatest was the joy in knowing that my Heavenly Father has really allowed me a share of work . . . I don't remember that there were many days of work neglected because of ill health."

It was indeed remarkable that she was able to do as much as she did. One who saw her in her work writes of the untiring enthusiasm and activity with which she gave herself to it: "Her work was her very life. She talked to me of her plans for the woman's school, and of her great desire to see a revival here in the schools. I am sure you know of her work last summer when the missionaries were all away—how, feeling that it was a mistake that the native Christians should be without the helps of divine worship and the weekly prayer meeting, she, with her sister's help, opened the church and held services all through the hot summer, *doing the preaching herself* and thus holding the people together. I never met any one at home or here whose whole soul was more on fire with a burning desire to win souls than was Anna Stone's, and I have met a large number of prominent workers in my work at home. She undoubtedly realized that her time was very short and she must work all the time while she had strength. Her work was not only in the school . . . but she was at work in the day schools and boarding schools, in the church, in the league, in the visitation, in the hospital—everywhere where her life was able to touch others; and one felt the influence of the Holy Spirit whenever in merest conversation with the girl. That happy smile and merry laugh that so won the hearts of the people at home were bestowed upon every one here, and I do not wonder she was able to reach hearts where others failed."

Her enthusiasm for her work doubtless made it hard not only for her to measure her own strength, but also for others to estimate it. But toward the close of the summer of 1905 it became evident to all, even to herself, that she had been overtaxing herself and must lighten her work. "Sister makes me take beef juice, milk, and bread and butter," she said in a letter to Mrs. Joyce. "Everybody tells me I am thin, but I am doing my best to get fat. Every afternoon I devote all the time to get well. I sleep after dinner, then go out riding for fresh air, so you see your little girl does live high and extravagantly."

During this summer she received news of the serious illness of her friend and foster-father, Bishop Joyce. This was a great source of anxiety and sorrow to her. "How I wish I had means to go right to his dear presence to tell him how I revere and love him for what he has done for me, and for what he is to the world," she wrote his wife. "I envy I-lien's privilege of being there. It must be a great comfort to be able to put one's heart-full of love and sympathy into little services that he may need at this time."

The death of this true friend was a great grief to her, both on her own account and because of the sorrow it brought to the family which she so loved. "I loved Bishop as I did my own father," she said in a letter to Mrs. Joyce. "Now I rejoice for both of them because they have heard the Master's 'Well done, good and faithful servant.'" Then she added, "I will ask him to ask the Master to let me work a little longer on earth. Of course if he sees the reason why I shouldn't he will not do it."

The Anna Stone Memorial

For a time it seemed as if her desire were to be granted, for when autumn came she was able to open the Women's School at the usual time, and to teach in it each morning. By keeping the afternoons free for rest she gained so much that she could write: "I feel very grateful for my health. I am up every day for my work. It is a busy life, but a very happy one." Dr. Stone had decided in the autumn that unless Anna gained a great deal within the next few weeks she would send her to the mountains for the winter, in the hope that the dry air would help her. But, as she said, "Anna hates to hear us talk about it because she does not want to leave her pet work." And Anna soon seemed so much stronger that the doctor did not insist on her going.

Anna wrote happily of the Christmas exercises in the school. "The women for the first time attempted to have a public programme for the happy season. They had a dialogue, three new songs, and acted out shepherds in the night watch and Herod in his trouble. Then they had a tree on which were little fancy trinkets which the women made for their friends. They had a joyous time because they worked for it." She carried the work until the Chinese New Year vacation, which began about the middle of January, and then dismissed the school for the vacation period, full of hopes and plans for the new term, for which she felt that the month's rest would prepare her. Special services were held in the church during the New Year vacation and Anna saved her strength that she might sing at the evening meetings. She herself led the closing service. One who was there says, "The native church will not quickly forget her clear and beautiful testimonies."

But her strength was not equal even to these tasks. Early in February she had a severe hemorrhage from her lungs, from which it seemed as if she could not rally. She felt this herself and said to Dr. Stone, with a brave smile, "Sister, I am going. This is in answer to prayer, for I do not want to linger on and endanger all of your lives." This attack was followed by pleurisy, and for ten days of severe suffering her life hung by a very slender thread. A fellow-worker wrote at this time: "She is bright and happy, although fully expecting to go. She has been so enthusiastic in her work, and always so cheerful, that she has often gone beyond her strength. I think that she has been failing more than we who daily watch her have realized. We feel that we cannot let her go, but it is not for us to say. Since she would rather go to God than stay and not be able to carry on her work, we can only pray 'The will of God be done.'"

Once more, however, she showed the elasticity which had made it so hard for her friends to realize the true state of her health, and for a few weeks seemed to improve. As life returned she began to hope that she might again be able to take up her work, and for a time the eagerness to work was so strong that she dreaded the thought of death. As the days passed and strength did not come, she was troubled to understand why, when the need was so great and the workers so few, she who so longed to work, should not be permitted to do so. She said to Dr. Stone one day: "Sister, I have just prepared myself to work, so much has been spent on me that I want to live at least fifteen years to pass on some of my blessings to others. I am so young, and our home life has been just beautiful. I am not anxious to give it up so soon. I have great hopes of the Training School. I love the women. I want to take a whole class through a course of training and then leave them with my work. I want to see them well established in their work, and a new school building put up well worthy of the name. Above all I want to see our native church thoroughly roused by the Holy Spirit, and a self-supporting church started."

One of the missionaries wrote afterward: "I wish you might have known what a comfort Dr. Stone was to her through all those dark hours, carrying her own burden constantly in her heart and yet bravely helping Anna to bear hers. And Anna on her side was just as brave, for she suffered intense pain through her illness, but constantly fought down every expression of it."

Anna's lifelong love for the will of God was so strong that she could not fail to love it to the end, and the struggle was soon succeeded by complete victory and peace. Her sister wrote Mrs. Joyce after she had gone: "She did not know why, when so much had been done for her and she was so willing to do any service unto the Lord, she should not be spared, and given a healthy body for the work that seemed to be so much in need of workers. But she said she was willing to go if it was the Lord's will, and she wanted people to know that she loved to obey God mare than she desired her own life . . . She said she was perfectly willing to go, only she had wanted to work a little longer."

Her brief struggle passed, her thought was all for others. She often spoke of the women for whom she had been working, and begged her sister to look after them and keep them from going back to the old ways; and in delirium she pleaded with one and another of them. She sent messages of love to those who were not with her, some of them being on the other side of the ocean, and sought to lighten the grief of those around her who so longed to keep her with them. "Do not grieve for me," she comforted her sister. "Think of me as you used to think of me when I was in America, only I shall be in a more beautiful place." Three days before her death she gave explicit directions about her funeral, wishing that everything in the Chinese funeral rites which savoured at all of non-Christian religions might be eliminated, that in her death, as in her life, she might witness clearly and unmistakably to her loyalty to Christ.

When the last call finally came, on the sixteenth of March, it found her ready and glad to respond. She told her sister that she had heard the beautiful music and seen the great light and wanted to go. "That evening," reads a letter from one of her co-workers, "we missionaries all gathered in the reception hall of their little house, together with her relatives and more intimate friends. It was one of the most touching scenes I have ever witnessed, for we were all drawn together by the bond of grief over the loss of one we loved."

Although, in accordance with Anna's wishes, her funeral was conducted with the utmost simplicity, the funeral procession caused universal comment. One of the missionaries describes the scene: "As the procession of almost forty chairs passed down the street all stopped to watch it pass, and despite the unrest due to the recent riots at Nanchang, we heard nothing but kindly remarks. The fact that foreigners were following one of their own people to the grave, paying the Chinese girl the honour they would have shown to a great man among themselves, seemed to impress the Chinese in a peculiar way."

Another writes: "During the day the neighbours, Christian and non-Christian alike, came to pay their respects . . . A very large company of people attended the funeral, including a number of missionaries of other denominations. There was a procession of forty sedan chairs to the Christian cemetery, which is about two miles beyond the East Gate. For the half mile from the home to the city gate both sides of the street were lined with people, who stood quietly and respectfully while we passed. The absence of the numerous heathen symbols, and of any cover for the casket save the floral tributes, was observed; and the fact that even the foreigners had their chairs draped with white, 'just like us Chinese,' was also noted. An English gentleman from the foreign concession, who was to pay a call on the captain of one of the war vessels the next morning, said, 'I shall tell him that I have witnessed a procession to-day which will do more to bring peace and harmony between the Chinese and foreigners than all the war vessels will do.'"

Measured by years, Anna Stone's life was short. Measured by the time which she was enabled to give to her work after her return to China, her service was brief. Almost all her life had been given to preparation for service, and it may seem as if she had hardly begun her life work when she was bidden to lay it down for the richer service of another life. But if to be is more than to do, and if Anna Stone's life be measured by what it was, rather than by achievements which could be recorded, we must count her years of service to have been many. Through all the years of preparation for her work she was, in fact, serving in the truest sense, through what she was. Bishop Joyce often said that her presence in the home was a benediction. One who had close contact with her work pays the following tribute:

> "Hers was a rare character. So simple, unaffected, and tender and yet withal so strong. Like the blameless knight of old, 'her strength was as the strength of ten because her heart was pure.' Gifted with a winsome personality, and a voice of great sweetness, she literally sang her way into the hearts of all who heard her, while the illumination of her life 'hid with Christ in God' particularly impressed those who saw in her a product of the missionary enterprise of our church. All who came within the influence of her radiant presence were the better for it."

Her life was an inspiration to people in Christian America. She once said while here: "Since coming to America the greatest wonder to me has been how any one can live in this country and yet not be a Christian. If I had not given myself to God it would be the first thing I would do. But thank God He has *me* off His mind. I am His child and I will love and serve Him all my days." One woman who heard her sing asked, "Why do you let her go back? We need her right here to help us. I never felt so near Christ as when I heard this Chinese girl sing, 'And I shall see Him face to face,' for the light of her vision shone from her eyes. I knew that she saw what she was singing about." Another wrote, when the news of her death came, "Of Anna Stone it can truthfully be said, 'None knew her but to love her.' . . . Wherever she mingled with people she drew them not only to herself, but to Christ. Eternity alone will reveal the many souls won to a Christian life through her influence."

At the annual meeting of the Woman's Foreign Missionary Society, held a few months after Anna Stone's death, the following resolution was unanimously adopted: "Resolved: That in memory of our dear Chinese girl, Anna Stone, we recall to your thought these words, applied to her by one who knew her well:

> 'And half we deemed she needed not
> The changing of her sphere
> To give to heaven a shining one
> Who walked an angel here.'"

Her life was a blessing to people in her own great country. Her sister wrote: "I am so thankful that she returned and spent about two years working for our own people. When I saw how much she was loved by the women and girls here I knew her short time with us had not been spent in vain." A letter from another Kiukiang worker says: "We felt when Miss Stone was taken from the Women's School that indeed its light and glory had departed. Her influence and life among the women will never be forgotten. Her gentleness, sweetness of spirit, and unselfishness, won a place in our hearts, and made us feel that we had caught a glimpse of the Master. Among her fellow-workers and her own people, she was universally beloved."

Miss Hughes, who was later appointed to take up the work which Anna had laid down, wrote in a letter to Mrs. Joyce: "I don't think any one will ever be able to tell you what a vacancy there is in Kiukiang since that little girl was taken from us. I was not in China any length of time before I, personally, realized something of the influence of her life. Her spirit of beautiful, consecrated young womanhood that so impressed every one at home seemed intensified when I saw her in the fall upon my arrival." Miss Hughes went on to tell of an incident which revealed what was doubtless one of the great sources of the power of the life that was so short in years. She says:

> "I think nothing that I have heard of Anna Stone's life speaks more clearly of the depth of real self-abnegation,— perfect obliteration of self, in fact—and the secret of her power in winning souls where others failed to win, than this story I am now to tell you. Several years ago, before Anna returned home from America, an old woman about sixty-four years of age, was engaged to do sewing for Dr. Stone from time to time. The woman was a widow with one son, who was an opium fiend in every sense of the word. He was unable to work, and deprived his mother of all the comforts, and often of the necessities of life, that he might buy opium."

> "One day the old woman was taken ill, and while ill, her son carried off the only clothes the old mother had (she slept with her clothes spread on top of the bed-clothes

as you know is the custom in China), and sold them for the miserable drug. The mother appealed to Dr. Stone, who took her, in her helpless, sick condition, into the hospital. As she grew well, she stayed on, doing such sewing as she could for her board, and in the hospital she heard for the first time of the 'Jesus doctrine.' Her hungry heart opened to the truth and she wanted to learn to read the Bible."

"One day, however, she came to the doctor and asked her if she thought if they prayed to God, He would save her son from his dreadful life. The doctor talked with her and found that the old woman was full of faith that it could be done. So they prayed about it, and a little while after, Dr. Stone gave the old woman money to take her son to the hospital for men in the city here and have the habit broken off. But the mother, instead of giving the man into the care of the authorities, and paying for his treatment herself, gave the money to the man, and he used it all in opium, being in a worse condition than ever."

"Some time later, due to the lack of funds, the hospital had to be closed for some time, but when it was reopened, the old mother pleaded that the son should be taken on as a coolie to work for his keep, and thus be out of temptation's way. He had been supplied again with money and put into the hospital, from which he came out apparently cured, but fell again. The plan for him to come to the hospital seemed to the doctor a rather dangerous one, for the man was a positive good-for-nothing. But in the meantime Anna had returned from America, and was, with her sister, willing to try him; for it seemed his last chance, and the mother had begged so hard for him. So he came to the hospital—a poor wretch, indeed, weak as a little child from the awful life he had lived."

"All opium was out of his reach here, and in a few days the absence of it showed by dreadful swelling of the limbs. He could not carry the smallest weight without great exertion, and the case seemed almost hopeless. But he gradually was broken from the use of the drug and was able to work about the place. Anna was using a sedan chair for her itinerating work, but she was so light that the coolies jolted her a great deal and hurt her; so she got her 'ricksha, and chose this poor wretch of a fellow, as her personal body-servant. When she went out on her evangelistic work, she had her mother with her, as you know, and this coolie went along drawing the 'ricksha. He became very devoted to her, and very carefully cared for her. When she had her meals with her mother, she had this coolie eat with her, lest he go off and get hold of opium. He is a very weak, easily led fellow, as you will have judged, and Anna felt his one safety was in keeping with them all the time. Little by little, the fellow straightened up and became stronger and able to do a respectable amount of work."

"Meantime Anna was teaching him, as she had opportunity, about Christ. Finally last New Year's Eve, at the watch-night service led by Anna herself, among those who openly took their stand for Christ, was this poor fellow. As far as we know he has led a straight life ever since. He is still working about the hospital and there is no sign of the old dissipation. When Anna left us a few weeks ago, the man's grief was great, and it was this old 'body-guard' who sat up all night the one night after the coffin was sealed and remained in the house. The old mother at sixty-seven years of age has learned to read the Bible and is a very earnest Christian."

"I wish I could tell you how it impressed me as Dr. Stone told of the efforts of Anna to win that poor wretch of a fellow to Christ. There wasn't a thing attractive about him, in fact, just the opposite; but she saw that there was a soul there to save, and with no apparent thought of herself, no shrinking from a man of his type, she, with the true spirit of the Lord she so closely followed, bent every effort to save him from the thing that had cursed his own and his mother's life. I think I have never heard anything more beautiful than this story of Anna, who with all the delicacy of her nature, her pure, sweet womanhood, her love of the refined that always marked her, and her keen sensitiveness to the niceties of life, laid all, as a sacrifice to her Lord, in the background, and had at the same board with herself and her mother, that miserable man, thus helping him to fight the enemy of his soul and body."

Her Master's work was indeed everything, and self was nothing to Anna Stone. She once said in a letter to Mrs. Joyce, "It has been a grief to my heart not to have seen more people who have means to support themselves come out to work for China. I am hoping to find some means by which to support myself without getting pay from the society, to let others know that I am not working for money, but for the love of God which is in my heart."

The influence of this young Chinese girl is but another witness to "the power of an endless life." She lives to-day in those whom she has inspired, and who seek to be as true as she.

BIBLIOBAZAAR

The essential book market!

Did you know that you can get any of our titles in large print?

Did you know that we have an ever-growing collection of books in many languages?

Order online:
www.bibliobazaar.com

Find all of your favorite classic books!

Stay up to date with the latest government reports!

At BiblioBazaar, we aim to make knowledge more accessible by making thousands of titles available to you- *quickly and affordably*.

Contact us:
BiblioBazaar
PO Box 21206
Charleston, SC 29413

LaVergne, TN USA
21 September 2009
158559LV00001B/128/A